Essentials in the Care and Conservation of Historical Ceramic Objects

Essentials in the Care and Conservation of Historical Ceramic Objects

Victoria L Oakley and Kamal K Jain

Archetype Publications

First published 2002 by Archetype Publications Ltd.

Archetype Publications Ltd.
6 Fitzroy Square
London W1T 5HJ

www.archetype.co.uk

Tel: 44 (207) 380 0800
Fax: 44 (207) 380 0500

All photographs courtesy of the V&A.

ISBN 1-873132-73-5

British Library Cataloguing in Publication Data
A catalogue record for this book is available from the British Library.

Typeset by Kate Williams, Abergavenny
Printed and bound in Great Britain by Henry Ling Ltd., The Dorset Press, Dorchester

Contents

Foreword

This publication is the outcome of a number of important and rewarding collaborations. The first is that between the Victoria and Albert Museum in London (V&A) and the Nehru Trust for the Indian Collections at the Victoria & Albert Museum (NTICVA) New Delhi. The NTICVA was set up as an independent trust in India in 1990 to provide greater access to the V&A's Indian collections and to increase the understanding and preservation of India's art and cultural heritage. The Trust provides awards for individual scholars and museum professionals in India and the UK to extend their study, research or training and to participate in collaborative ventures in these fields. The V&A itself, which hosts a steady flow of visiting colleagues from India, not only houses some of the most important and historic holdings of the arts of the South Asian subcontinent outside India, but also holds one of the world's richest and most extensive collections of ceramics.

The second collaboration is that between two dedicated conservators – Kamal K Jain of the National Research Laboratory for Conservation, Lucknow, India, who spent three months at the V&A in 1994 under the auspices of the NTICVA, and Victoria Oakley of the V&A, with whom he worked. Their aim was to produce a basic publication on ceramics conservation, appropriate to a wide audience of curators and conservators.

The third, and equally critical, collaboration is that between the authors and Jim Black of Archetype Publications, whose initial encouragement and subsequent adoption of the project has brought it into the public domain.

Both the V&A and the NTICVA are delighted to have played a role in contributing to the creation of this volume, which will certainly increase awareness of the need to preserve the world's rich ceramic heritage.

Deborah Swallow
Director of Collections, V&A
Executive Trustee, NTICVA

Acknowledgements

The seed that inspired the creation of this publication was first planted by Kamal K. Jain in 1994 during a three month internship in the Ceramics and Glass Conservation Section at the Victoria and Albert Museum (V&A), London, generously funded by the Nehru Trust for the Indian Collections at the V&A (NTICVA). In 1996, a study tour, supported by the V&A Research Committee, to various conservation laboratories in India, was undertaken by Victoria Oakley to confirm the need for such a publication.

As with any publication, a number of individuals have played vital roles and contributed to the final result. The authors would particularly like to extend their very warm thanks to Dr Deborah Swallow, Keeper, Asian Department (V&A) and Executive Trustee of the NTICVA, for her constant encouragement and enthusiasm throughout the project from its inception to the final conclusion. The authors also gratefully acknowledge the support and encouragement given by: Dr Jonathan Ashley-Smith, Head of Conservation (V&A), Dr Tej Singh, Director National Research Laboratory for Conservation (NRLC), Lucknow and Shri Atul Kumar Yadav, Junior Scientific Officer, NRLC, Lucknow. Various colleagues, who kindly agreed to read the draft text and contributed comments and advice on content included Senior Ceramic and Glass Conservators (V&A) Fi Jordan and Juanita Navarro, and Graham Parlett, Curator, Indian and South East Asian Section (V&A). The authors are also indebted to Peter Ford, Applications Support Manager, Information Systems Services Department (V&A) for his patience in interpreting instructions for diagrams and for his advice and input on format. Paul Robins, Photographer, Photographic Services Department (V&A) must also be thanked for his contribution to the photography. Last but by no means least, Kamal K. Jain wishes to thank his wife Dr Beena Jain for her patience and fortitude during the period he was away from India studying in the UK.

Preface

Ceramic objects form a substantial part of collections in museums all over the world, India and South-east Asia being no exception. The survival of large numbers of ancient ceramic objects might suggest that these inorganic materials are relatively durable, and that they do not demand the same level of care that is regarded as essential to objects derived from other types of material. However, all composite materials, including ceramics, are, to a greater or lesser extent, vulnerable to decay and require proper care and conservation treatment to safeguard them for posterity. Inappropriate environments, careless handling and unsuitable treatments can bring about the deterioration of these objects.

The last two to three decades have seen the growth of ceramics conservation as a specialised subject. Museum professionals have become increasingly aware that any attempt to undertake ceramic conservation work without adequate knowledge or expertise may cause further problems. Unfortunately, the growth of ceramic conservation world-wide has not been consistent. In countries where resources for conservation are limited, the emphasis on the care and conservation of cultural heritage has, understandably, tended to rest with those objects that are most vulnerable to hostile environmental conditions. Consequently, the preservation of ceramics has been regarded largely as a low and generally ignored. It seems that it is only when their condition becomes acute that they merit the conservator's attention, and by then it may be too late to save them. Any well-intended intervention by a non-specialist at this stage may be inappropriate and do more harm than good. With greater awareness such situations can be avoided, and the additional investment of a conservator's time to extend his/her knowledge may prove more economical in the long term.

The published literature on the subject is wide and varied, ranging from conference proceedings describing detailed research projects through to books that are intended for the hobbyist. Access to these publications can be difficult for conservators working outside Europe and the USA. This small book aims to provide a basic methodology for the care and conservation of historical ceramics for professionals working in museum collections in relative isolation. However, it must be emphasised that treatment of an object without adequate knowledge may inadvertently result in damage, so while carrying out any treatment a cautious approach is necessary. If there is any doubt as to how best to proceed, the advice of an expert should always be sought.

CHAPTER ONE

Ceramic technology

Almost all ceramic objects are derived from clay, a material that is abundantly available on the surface of the earth. There are of course a small number of exceptions, for example quartz-rich Egyptian faience and other stone-paste or fritware bodies. The raw clay is extracted from the ground, prepared, then formed into objects, dried and finally fired. These stages form the essential process required to make a ceramic or pottery artefact. Such an approach was known to early man from before Neolithic times; the evidence has survived as testament both to those early civilisations and to the sheer endurance of the ceramic medium itself. Within this basic method there is a myriad of ways in which the clay can be worked and subsequently decorated. Indeed, the versatile properties of clay have allowed it to find applications in science, industry and architecture, as well as in a decorative and domestic context.

An awareness of the materials and processes involved in producing ceramics is fundamental to the decision-making process of the ceramics conservator when considering treatments. Similarly, the deterioration of ceramics can be related generally to the materials and techniques used and the resulting physical properties of the fired object. Familiarity and understanding, through either the actual practice of the craft itself or by the detailed examination and study of the objects themselves, provides an invaluable background to appreciating the scope and limitations of the ceramic medium.

What is clay?

In scientific terms clay can be described as a hydrated silicate of aluminium. It consists of finely divided particles derived from a complex process involving the gradual decomposition of igneous and metamorphic rocks on the earth's crust. During the course of millions of years of intensive weathering, the basic constituents of the rocks – feldspar, quartz and mica – are eventually ground down into clay. Those clays found where they are formed are referred to as primary or residual clays, while those that are later transported by natural agents such as rivers, glaciers and seas, undergoing further prolonged decomposition, are known as secondary or sedimentary clays.

The main product of the weathering process, and the most important constituent of the clay, is the mineral kaolinite. It has a layered structure consisting of hexagonal plate-like particles that are capable of retaining water. Kaolinite is regarded as the idealised clay mineral, and although it is the ingredient common to all clays, it never occurs in its pure state. Generally, clays will contain many other ingredients including quartz, feldspar, flint, fillers and impurities such as iron oxides, titanium dioxide and organic materials.

The very small size of the clay platelets, together with their shape, causes water to cling to the surface of each particle, attracted by chemical and physical forces. The film of moisture surrounding each particle, while causing the plates to stick together also lubricates them. This property makes the clay plastic when moist: the plates slip and slide when pressure is applied allowing the clay to be formed into shapes as desired. The shape hardens upon drying as the water evaporates but can be softened again with the application of water. However, when dried clay is heated to temperatures in excess of 600°C, various irreversible changes take place in the composition and structure of clay during the firing process. The fired body is hard and brittle and can no longer be softened by water. The ability of the fired body to absorb water is related to the final firing temperature of the object: the higher the temperature the less porous the body.

The nature of clay bodies

Naturally occurring clays are rarely used on their own since they seldom have a suitable composition to perform satisfactorily during forming, firing and use of the object. For a clay to be usable it should possess three important properties: (1) it should have sufficient plasticity to allow the potter to form the object by his/her chosen technique; (2) it must possess porosity in order that moisture can escape and so avoid warping and cracking prior to firing; and (3) it requires a refractory nature so that objects made from it can endure the firing without distortion.

The clay bodies are prepared according to calculated mixtures of clay combined with fluxes, hardeners and openers. The clay component in the body may be a blend of several different types of clay such as ball clay, china clay and fire clay, each possessing distinct properties. The fluxes melt during the firing to form a glass-like material which flows into the small spaces thus fusing the tiny particles together. Examples of fluxes include feldspatic materials and alkaline earth metal oxides. The hardeners are forms of silica (e.g., flint, quartz and sand) which are fluxed during the firing and impart hardness to the resulting structure. Openers, such as grog, fire clay and organic material, provide texture and workability.

Preparation involves mechanically grinding the clay down with water. The increased potential points of contact between the smaller particles result in improved strength. Sieving and stirring the clay creates a homogenous mix. Excess water is removed by filtration and air is expelled during wedging, which is the repeated slicing and thrusting together of lumps of clay to improve consistency.

Red clays are usually fired at comparatively low temperatures (around 1000°C). They contain a high proportion of iron (around 5–8%) causing the resulting wares to be coloured shades of orange to red. Red clays tend to be highly plastic, having very finely ground particles due to intensive weathering during their formation. Deposits of this type are common and, consequently, have been used through the ages for utilitarian wares such as slipware, tiles, flowerpots and bricks.

Ball clays possess such high plasticity that they are not suitable for use on their own. To avoid poor drying and risk of warping and contraction, they tend to be mixed with other clays such as white earthenware to which they give plasticity. They fire to a cream colour at around 1300°C.

China clays (kaolin) have very little plasticity; other clays such as ball clay are added in order to make them workable. China clay is the purest naturally occurring clay. It is one of the main ingredients in porcelain and white earthenware bodies to which it is added to impart whiteness and control their firing properties.

Fire clays are refractory and fire to around 1500°C, resulting in a buff colour. They are relatively plastic and are used to make refractory articles such as crucibles and furnace linings. They form an important basis for stoneware bodies.

Ceramic wares

Pottery is generally divided into three broad categories that relate to the temperature at which the clay is fired: earthenware, stoneware and porcelain. The divisions between each category are not sharply defined and it should be remembered that conservators may occasionally encounter objects made of clay which have not been fired, but merely baked in the sunshine.

Earthenware

The term earthenware describes pottery fired at lower temperatures (up to around 1150°C). Heating the clay up to higher temperatures risks deformation and causes weaknesses. The particles in the fired clay are only partly fused giving rise to spaces or pores and hence the typical porous (and weak) nature of earthenware pottery. This aspect has implications for conservation in several important ways since liquids will be drawn easily into the pores to cause staining. Glaze applied to the surface, usually in a second firing (below 1100°C), provides a protective, hygienic and waterproof layer that also strengthens the ware. The low temperature of the glaze firing offers scope for bright colours produced by the metal-based colouring agents. The bond between the glaze and the body tends to be weak, and in section under magnification appears as a distinct surface layer. Earthenware vessels are usually potted with thicker walls compared to other wares, in order to compensate for the relative lack of strength in the fired clay structure (Fig.1.1).

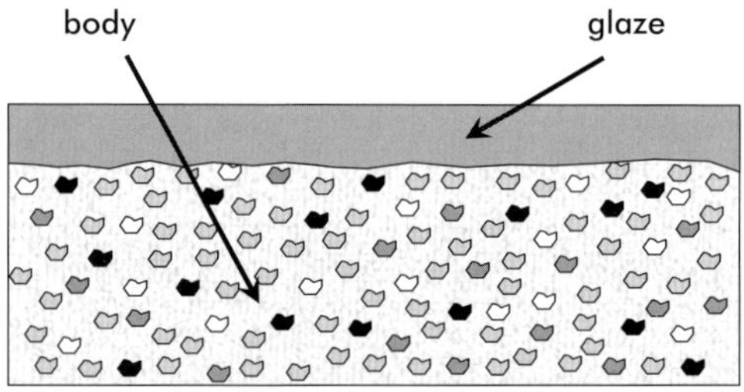

Figure 1.1 Section through an earthenware body. The body is coarse with open pores and small inclusions. The glaze is visible as a distinct layer over the body.

Stoneware

Stoneware is usually fired to temperatures above 1200°C and differs from earthenware by being vitrified. This means that the pores or spaces between the solid particles are almost completely filled by a glassy phase, rendering the ware virtually non-porous. The glaze and body are also well integrated resulting in a strong hard body that is impermeable to liquids. These qualities influence the types of deterioration as well as the conservator's choice in materials and techniques for treatment (Fig. 1.2).

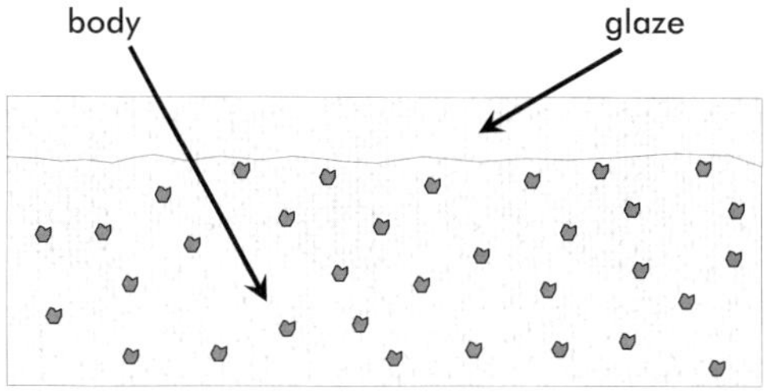

Figure 1.2 Section through a stoneware body. The body is dense and more vitrified than earthenware, with less impurities and air spaces. The glaze and body are closely fused.

Porcelain

Porcelain can be regarded as a type of stoneware and includes wares that are white and translucent. It is extremely hard and non-porous having been fired to a temperature above 1300°C. It should be mentioned that there are several types of porcelain, the clay bodies are composed of mixtures of clay which are often less plastic than earthenware or stoneware. Hard-paste porcelain or true porcelain differs from soft-paste porcelain in composition; soft-paste containing more flux to allow a lower temperature firing resulting in a more brittle body with slight porosity (Fig. 1.3).

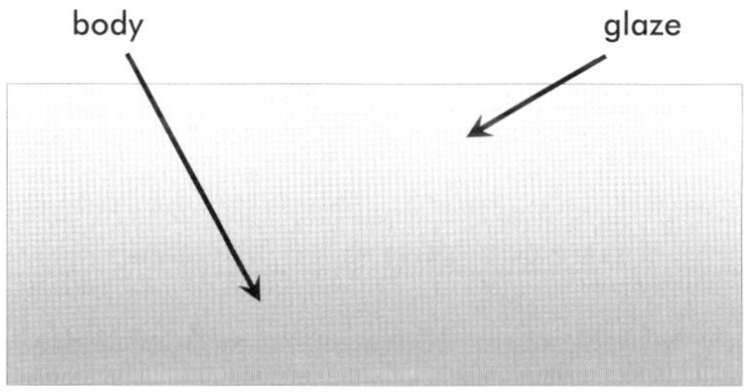

Figure 1.3 Section through a porcelain body. The body is glassy and highly vitrified with an intimately fused glaze.

Fabrication methods

Several thousands of years of continuing the tradition of pottery making has resulted in a gradual evolution in fabrication and firing techniques. While some of the most primitive methods are still used by practising potters today to make individual objects, highly mechanised industrial processes are now commonplace in the mass production of everyday domestic wares.

The simplest approach, involving hand-building and freehand shaping, relies on only a few tools. Clay is pinched by the fingers to create a vessel form or pinch pot. To make a coil-pot a long snake of clay is worked around in a spiralling configuration, integrating each round with the previous lower layer. Slab-pots are formed from sheets of leather-hard clay joined together.

The use of moulds allows potential for mass production. Soft clay is pressed against a mould specially made from absorbent material such as plaster of Paris or low-fired earthenware. The clay is left to dry until leather-hard, and at this point it is easily removed from the mould and finished off, joining components from different moulds together as necessary. Another approach to moulding involves the use of fluid clay, or slip, which is poured into the mould, the thickness of the cast being determined by the length of time lapsed before pouring away the remaining slip.

The art of throwing dates back to before 4000 BC. The technique is used for repeated production of symmetrical vessel forms using a revolving turn-table or wheel. The process requires a highly plastic clay which is applied as a lump to the flat surface of the wheel and by exerting controlled pressure with two hands, a form is coaxed up out of the clay.

The processes of jollying and jiggering – methods for mass producing large quantities of uniformly sized cups, saucers and plates – can be described as a mechanical form of throwing. A mould is lined with clay of medium plasticity and revolved while a profile is brought towards the mould simultaneously pressing and cutting away the excess clay. Jiggers are used for making flatware such as plates, while jollies make ceramic vessels such as cups.

Decoration and glaze

There are numerous possibilities for decorating and embellishing ceramic objects, and the processes by which these are achieved can occur at any stage during the fabrication. The simplest and most immediate result can be obtained using a tool to incise, cut or impress a mark on the soft clay. Raised decoration can also be achieved at this stage by modelling or through the use of moulds where decorative components are moulded and then applied to the object's surface. Other effects may also be obtained with coloured slips using techniques such as trailing, marbling and combing. Slip can be inlaid into impressions or incisions in the surface of the unfired object. Decoration can also be created using unfired paints. Occasionally, in order to make the surface of an earthenware object less porous, the surface is sealed using organic materials such as waxes, milk, fat and lacquers.

Typically one imagines the most important decorative stage to be the application of the glaze – a layer of glass applied to the surface of the ware. Besides decoration, it serves to strengthen the object and provides an impermeable hygienic layer. A glaze can be made more interesting by the addition of colour, achieved through the addition of metallic compounds. Metallic ions can bring about various effects in combination with other materials and under different firing conditions. Colours can be applied in one of three main ways:

1. **Underglaze colours** – colours can be applied to the porous biscuit surface after the object has received its first firing; the colour is then sealed in place by the application of a glaze on top. In some cases the colour may even be applied to unfired ware and the glaze then applied over, either before or after the first firing. The colours are achieved by the direct painting of the metallic oxides in a medium on the ceramic surface. Alternatively, through the indirect use of printing techniques, a print can be transferred onto the object. Such colours applied under the glaze tend to be less vulnerable to deterioration since they are protected by the overlying glaze.
2. **In-glaze colours** – the metallic colour-producing compounds may be incorporated in the glaze recipe thus producing colour within the glaze itself. Alternatively the colour may be painted onto the unfired glaze similar to the way that an artist uses a blank sheet of paper.
3. **On-glaze or overglaze colours** – after the stoneware, earthenware or porcelain object has been glazed and fired, there are still further possibilities for decorating. Metal oxides in the form of enamels and lustres can be painted or transferred onto the glaze. An additional though much lower temperature firing is necessary (600–900°C) to fuse them onto the glaze. However, because of the lower temperature firing and the materials which they contain, on-glaze decoration tends to be less resistant to wear. On ancient and historic pieces it is often the on-glaze decoration – particularly lustres and gilding – that shows signs of wear and loss first.

Firing

Except perhaps in the case of some ethnographic pottery, the ceramic object will have to be subjected to firing at least once during the production. The firings are critical in determining the nature of the resulting ceramic and must follow a sequence of controlled stages culminating in the carefully monitored cooling of the wares. Typically, the production of an object will involve a biscuit firing then a glaze firing, sometimes followed by further lower temperature firings for on-glaze colours.

The remaining water in the clay has to be driven off carefully in order to avoid the risk of explosions. The temperature of the kiln is slowly raised until the boiling point of water temperature has been reached. At this stage most of the trapped water will have evaporated away. Water combined chemically, at a molecular level, escapes by around 600°C. The clay will be irreversibly changed in its crystalline structure. Just before 900°C the carbonaceous matter is burned out; it is important that this stage is fully complete otherwise blisters of trapped gas may occur.

Every time a ceramic object undergoes heating or cooling, a reversible alteration occurs at 573°C involving the molecular rearrangement of the crystalline structure of the quartz accompanied by a slight (2%) increase in volume. Unless this stage is carefully controlled cracks may result. At around 800°C the process of vitrification starts to occur: melted fluxes and silica start to melt and fuse. Further rises in temperature continue the complex alteration of the various clay minerals.

The point at which the firing process is stopped greatly affects the physical properties of the final ware. In reality, the type of clay will generally determine the final firing temperature. The potter's choice of clay depends on the type of object s/he is making; for example, fine delicate translucent teacups would suggest a porcelain clay, whereas a functional flowerpot would be less suited to such a choice.

The atmosphere surrounding the object during firing will also affect its final appearance. If there is a plentiful supply of air, and hence an abundance of oxygen, the atmosphere is described as oxidising. The opposite is a reducing or oxygen-starved atmosphere caused by an excess of fuel and a smoky fire. Metal oxides are affected by the amount of oxygen present with the result that different colours are produced, for example, iron oxides form red hematite in oxidising conditions, while in reduction black magnetite is formed and carbon may remain in the body.

With the exception of unfired sun-baked ceramics, all ceramics will, at some point, have been heated to high temperatures. While some domestic wares may also experience high temperatures during their use, generally it is regarded by conservators as extremely unwise to subject historic or archaeological objects to further heating. The reasons for this include the risk of causing or accentuating any weaknesses through thermal expansion and contraction, and also the risk of loss of information that might be gained through analysis such as thermoluminescence testing, which is used to determine the age of fired ceramics.

CHAPTER TWO

Types of deterioration in ceramics

It is the nature of all composite materials eventually to become degraded into their basic constituents. The degradation usually occurs as a result of reactions with factors either in the environment or between elements or compounds from which the object is made. In the case of ceramics, deterioration is due almost exclusively to environmental factors – most commonly mechanical deterioration, the process being comparatively rapid where it occurs. Chemical deterioration, while less common, tends to be slower.

The physical properties of ceramics can vary enormously depending on several variables involved in their manufacture. These include the raw materials, fabrication techniques and firing. All these factors are responsible for determining the strength and durability of an object and predict the extent of physical vulnerability which all ceramic objects share to a greater or lesser degree. As a general rule, lower-fired ceramics deteriorate much more easily than those that are fired to a higher temperature.

Within museums and private collections there should be no need for a ceramic object to deteriorate, except in rare circumstances. Ceramics are probably one of the most stable groups of decorative artefacts. Archaeology testifies to this fact and illustrates how, under certain conditions, ceramic objects can endure for thousands of years.

In the normal domestic or museum environment, the greatest threat to ceramics is undoubtedly humans. Unfortunately it is not possible to guarantee that an object will be maintained in the same pristine condition as the day it was made. More usually the object will have been affected by one of the following:

- accumulation of dirt
- physical deterioration
- chemical deterioration.

Disfigurement caused by dirt and staining

Superficial dirt and stains can disfigure an object especially if the main purpose of the object is to be decorative. Deposits of unwanted material may just be confined to the surface of the object, but if the ceramic is porous – as in the case of low-fired earthenwares – then material may be carried in solution deep into the pores. It is important to also note that in the case of certain archaeological and ethnographic ceramics, such foreign material may provide interesting information about the object's original context. Dirt and staining may arise for a variety of reasons associated with earlier use or environmental factors.

Food stains

Earthenware vessels and dishes that have been used for food preparation can become stained due to foodstuffs seeping through flaws in a normally impermeable glaze (e.g., cracks, chips, pin holes, crazing). Greasy staining may be particularly bad if the vessel has been heated and any flaws in the glaze will be emphasised.

Metal staining

One of the more common types of staining is caused by metals. This may occur in pottery that has been buried or may arise from previous restoration techniques involving the use of metal mounts or supports that have subsequently corroded (Fig. 2.1).

Porous ceramics that have been buried in soils in which iron oxides are present may acquire iron stains that are extremely difficult to remove, a problem that can be further exacerbated by contact with other materials such as tannic acid from decaying vegetable matter. If ceramics have been buried with assorted metal objects the resulting deposits and staining should be retained as important archaeological evidence.

Encrustations

Encrustations may occur when a vessel has been in contact with water for prolonged periods – either in use or from burial causing the build-up of lime deposits. These are also found in ceramic oil lamps, objects from a marine environment and tiles that have been in an architectural context.

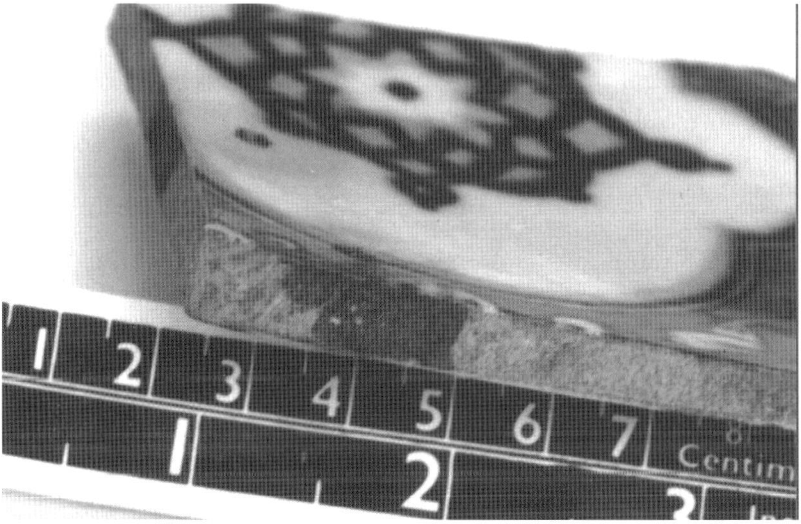

Figure 2.1 Fragment of earthenware object with stains caused by the absorption of corrosion products from iron rivets which have now been removed.

Museum dust and dirt

Particles of dust from the surrounding environment will gradually settle on the surface of objects and may, over time, cause disfigurement and damage depending on the degree of penetration. Particulate pollutants derived from the combustion of fossil fuels by vehicles in urban areas – as well as small particles of skin, clothing and building materials – can all gradually accumulate on exposed surfaces.

Mould growth

In conditions of high humidity, spores of mould normally found in the atmosphere may start to grow on organic residues present on the surface or in the pores of a porous pot.

Deposits and stains from fire

The accumulation of particulate contaminants generated by combustion of organic fuels may cause superficial disfigurement of the surface of an object.

Repair materials

Materials used in the treatment of objects may, for one reason or another, be unintentionally (or intentionally) deposited over areas other than those where they are required. Examples of this include instances where adhesive has been smeared over break edges, salts remaining as a result of acid cleaning treatments, and residues left behind from the use of pressure-sensitive adhesive tapes. Spraying and airbrush work can extend to an unacceptable amount over the intact glaze or body and, when disfigured or discoloured by ageing, may become unsightly (Fig. 2.2).

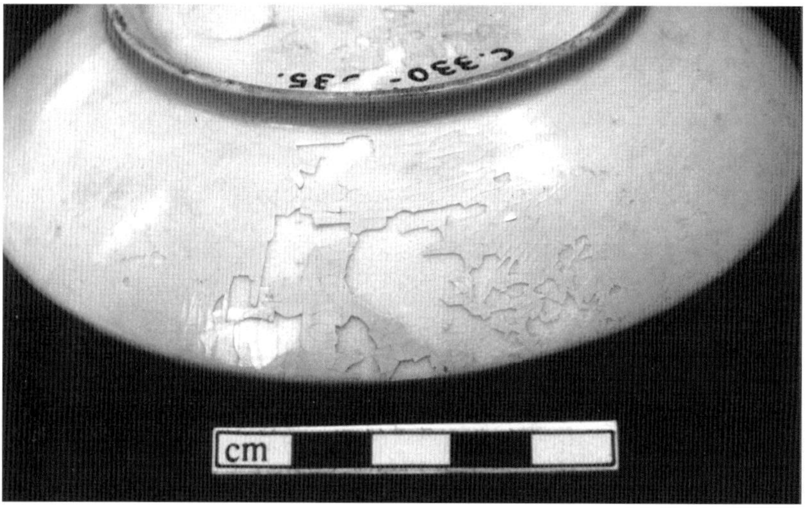

Figure 2.2 The surface of an object partially obscured and disfigured by over paint.

Mechanical or physical deterioration

After dirt and staining, physical damage is probably the next most common form of deterioration to ceramics. Their fragility causes them to be very susceptible to mechanical shock.

Manufacturing defects

Strictly speaking this should form a category of its own, although the general consequence of it is usually some form of physical damage. It is an inbuilt condition that predisposes the object to failure. There may be any number of different causes, but the most common stem from one of the following: a poorly formulated body or glaze; poor design or construction; inappropriate or uncontrolled firing.

It is also important that the clay has been formulated so that it is appropriate to the function of the object (e.g., ovenware). A body that contains inadequate amounts of filler and that has been allowed to dry too rapidly may well crack; and if the same body is fired too rapidly it could break.

Clay that has not been allowed to dry properly before firing can, in extreme cases, explode in the kiln through generation of steam in its pores. Unless heating and cooling of the kiln are carefully controlled, cracks known as dunts may occur – particularly if the body contains too much quartz.

The development of strain in a glaze can cause a network of superficial cracks through the glaze (but not the body) known as crazing. This is the result of the coefficient of expansion and contraction of the glaze not being compatible with that of the body. This may be apparent as the object emerges from the kiln or it may develop later during use where repeated heating and cooling causes stresses that are released by crazing. Ideally, the coefficient of expansion of the glaze should be slightly less than that of the body so that the glaze is under compression. Peeling of glazes (also known as shivering or scaling) may occur for the opposite reasons to crazing, i.e. the glaze contracts less on cooling than the underlying body. This results in poor adhesion of glaze to body causing sections of glaze to flake away. The fault is usually due to relatively large proportions of quartz in the body so that the body shrinks more than is appropriate for the glaze.

Composite forms, such as figure groups and the handles on cups, are often made by assembling, or luting, the various parts together when the clay is leather-hard. The area of attachment may be weak if the joins have not been carefully made. Also, if an object is of an impractical design (e.g., some modern sculptures) this may contribute to its vulnerability.

Impact damage

Impact is probably the most obvious and common cause of damage to ceramics. Either by accident or through carelessness, a sudden collision between the ceramic and a more resistant material has resulted in chipping, cracking or breakage, directly or indirectly as a result of human intervention. Conservation can unintentionally bring about impact damage as a result of using excessive force, for example, the use of hammers and chisels to remove mortar from the back of tiles.

Abrasion

Abrasion may have occurred through use (e.g., to plates and bowls from eating implements) or harsh cleaning methods. The practice of stacking plates can produce scratches caused by the rough unglazed foot grinding at the glazed surface. Conservation methods can also cause unintended abrasion when unwanted accretions or excess fills are removed using scalpels, abrasives, files, riflers or dental burrs.

Generally lower-fired, and hence softer, bodies and glazes are more susceptible to damage of this kind. Gilding, lustres and enamel decoration are particularly vulnerable as they are fired at much lower temperatures.

Thermal shock damage

If sudden warming or cooling occurs this can be sufficient to cause uneven rates of expansion or contraction of the glaze and body so that stresses occur, resulting in cracks or breaks. This is generally associated with domestic use.

Soluble salts

If water-soluble salts are absorbed by a porous body these can pose a threat to the object, particularly if the surrounding environmental conditions are unstable. Recrystallisation of the salts, in dry conditions, will cause damage as the crystals tend to occupy a greater volume than while in solution.

This phenomenon – which may take the form of a regular cycle during wet and dry periods, especially during the monsoon and summer seasons – results in tremendous pressures within the pores of the ceramic or at the glaze–body interface. Pressures may be sufficient to push the surface apart or cause a glaze to flake away. The speed at which crystallisation occurs is dependent on ambient temperature and relative humidity (RH): the faster it occurs the more damaging the effect. This is a particular problem with earthenware tiles that have been in an architectural context (Fig. 2.3), storage vessels and archaeological objects from either marine or land excavations. Generally, the typical salts will be chlorides, nitrates, phosphates and sulphates.

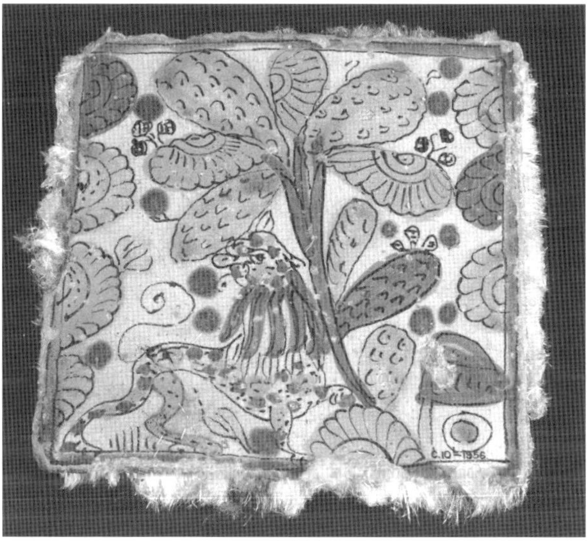

Figure 2.3 Glazed earthenware tile from Mexico with salt efflorescence on unglazed edges.

Compression damage

In the case of ceramics that have been buried, the pressure of the earth above may cause the object to break.

Frost damage

In countries that have long winter periods of sub-zero temperatures, frost damage may occur. The cause of the damage is the formation of ice in the pores of the ceramic resulting in the surface spalling away from the body.

Root action

Pottery that has become softened through burial in wet conditions may not be strong enough to resist the penetration of roots. This occurs in the case of cremation urns buried in acid soil, where the plant roots grow towards the nutrient-rich material in the urns.

Chemical deterioration

This type of deterioration is less common in ceramics. Minor chemical deterioration may occasionally occur during use, but major chemical deterioration is generally found only in ceramics that have been subjected to extreme conditions, for example, when buried or subjected to accidental fire.

Water

In wet conditions, ceramics that have been low fired to temperatures around 600°C may rehydrate, resulting in deformation or disintegration. Unfired decoration will also be at severe risk from water contact. Higher-fired earthenwares with the soluble components gypsum (hydrated calcium sulphate) and calcite (calcium carbonate) may gradually dissolve. Extended soaking during a conservation treatment – e.g., when removing soluble salts – can cause similar dissolution of soluble components.

Acid attack

Conservation treatments may occasionally involve the use of strong acids, for example when removing iron stains. There is the risk that calcareous fillers in the body may be attacked and reactions may occur with components in the body. Acidic ground water in contact with buried ceramics can result in calcareous components being dissolved; certain glazes and glass may also be attacked and degraded.

Ceramics in constant daily use may be attacked by acids in food. The degree of attack from these may be so small as to be immeasurable, but certain glazes can be attacked to such a degree that toxic amounts of metallic components are dissolved out of the fired glaze (e.g., selenium, barium, zinc, cadmium, antimony and lead). Stoneware and porcelain glazes are less liable to attack owing to the absence of metal fluxes and the extra resistance provided by their high silica content.

Alkaline attack

This is more likely to affect the glaze of a ceramic than the body. The deterioration of glass, and hence glazes, is faster in alkaline conditions than acid ones. Alkalis are leached from the glassy matrix and in extreme cases the colloidal silica can become dissolved. Iridescence may result due to the way in which light is reflected from the laminating surface and ultimately the surface may exfoliate. The colouring of glazes may also be affected through the leaching of alkalis.

Lead sulphide blackening

This is fairly unusual but may occur in ceramics that have been buried. Under certain anaerobic conditions where air is absent, decaying plant and animal tissues allow a group of bacteria to thrive that can be extremely damaging to lead glazes. The bacteria generate hydrogen sulphide as part of their metabolic process and this reacts with the lead in the glaze to yield a black insoluble lead sulphide.

Sequestration

Sequestering agents are present in some commercial cleaning agents (e.g., domestic washing powders, dish washing powders). These may affect high-lead glazes and on-glaze decoration. Burial in association with animal bones may result in deterioration of lead glazes due to the release of phosphate ions from the bone which may form sequestering compounds.

Alteration due to fire

The stability of ceramics as a class of objects may be attributed to a great extent to the fact that they are subjected to very high temperatures during their manufacture. However, if they are then reheated to a similar temperature, changes in the molecular make-up may take place. The temperature at which any changes may occur is related directly to the firing temperatures of any particular part of the object. Therefore on-glaze decoration which is fired at much lower temperatures will be particularly vulnerable. Any unfired decoration may be burned away and completely destroyed. Also the final appearance will be affected by the amount of oxygen in the atmosphere of the fire.

CHAPTER THREE

Care of ceramic objects

It would be a mistake to assume that the most important aspects of the ceramics conservator's work involve the *active* treatment of objects. Possibly even more important is the non-interventive approach involving the *preventive* care of the objects. Such an approach entails protecting the object from the threat of decay by controlling various factors in the surrounding environment.

The first two chapters described how the physical properties of ceramic objects are determined by the materials and processes used in their manufacture, and how these properties may also be linked to the various types of damage an object may sustain when exposed to harsh or inappropriate conditions. An understanding of the processes that most commonly bring about the deterioration of ceramic objects will greatly assist the conservator in minimising the risks from potential sources of damage.

Environmental factors during storage and display

Unlike most other types of objects, ceramics are comparatively less susceptible to factors in the museum environment.

Temperature

Extremes of temperature can harm ceramics by causing thermal shock or by weakening existing faults. For this reason it is unwise to subject ceramics to high or low temperatures, as for example in an oven or freezer. Even placing ceramics in hot sunshine on a windowsill can weaken an existing fault. Restored ceramics are especially vulnerable: this includes recently restored pieces which should not be subjected to high temperatures. Certain types of adhesive soften when heated, while others may discolour and age more rapidly.

Light

Unless the ceramic has an unfired decorative surface, light levels should not present a problem. However, if an object has been restored, the synthetic resins that have been used to fill, bond and retouch the surface may become more yellow in bright light. Conversely, some retouching media will discolour in the dark (Fig. 3.1).

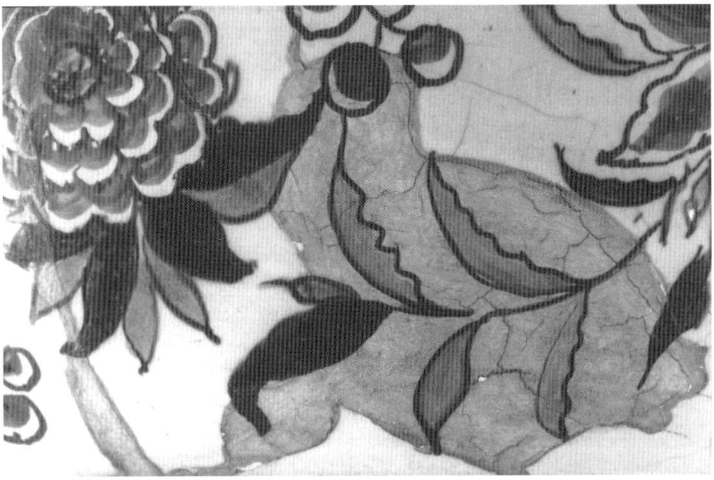

Figure 3.1 Areas of retouching discoloured as a result of ageing.

Humidity

Changes in the moisture content of the air are not normally a threat to ceramics except if there are other water-sensitive materials in close association with the ceramic. Generally, an RH within the range 40–65% is considered acceptable for sound ceramic objects. This may not be the case for objects that have metal mounts, rivets and dowels as these components can be susceptible to corrosion in high humidity. Any ceramics containing deliquescent salts may be very sensitive to changes in humidity. Mould growth may occur in particular situations such as organic material in contact with the ceramic. Old plaster fillings used to replace missing areas on damaged ceramics can also cause problems in high humidity. Salts from the plaster, particularly sulphates, may be absorbed into porous ceramic. If a water-soluble adhesive has been used to repair ceramics, those objects should always be kept dry.

It is important to keep a regular record of temperature and RH data in display and storage areas, particularly those that contain vulnerable objects. This can be achieved by installing a simple device such as a thermohygrograph which can be checked on a weekly basis. In areas that suffer from excessive, unacceptable levels of RH, it is advisable to control it through the use of silica gel inside the storage cabinets.

Pollution

Dust and dirt may be present in the air in varying concentrations depending on the location. Such contaminants, which can be highly alkaline, may disfigure ceramics temporarily or permanently depending upon the degree

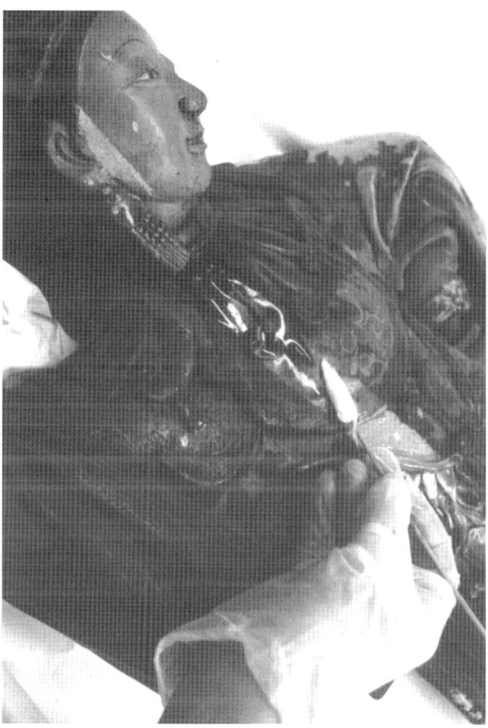

Figure 3.2 Object with surface disfigured by layer of dirt undergoing cleaning.

of penetration and the nature of the pollutant (Fig. 3.2). Volatile organic pollutants arising from the offgassing of wooden storage cabinets can interact with ceramics giving rise to calclacite salts. Archaeological ceramics that have been cleaned previously using acid treatments may be particularly vulnerable to this type of salt growth.

Vibration

A springy floor or local road or rail traffic may give rise to vibration and can lead to damage – either directly by abrasion and wear causing loss of the surface or glaze, or by objects creeping (slowly moving), especially on hard surfaces. This may even lead to an object dropping off a shelf. Where this is a serious threat to objects, shelves should have raised lips attached to their edges. Alternatively, objects should be placed on a small mat of a material that will offer resistance to such movement (such as chamois, felt or silicone rubber), or attached to the surface with an appropriate adhesive or a wax composition.

Human intervention

Handling and moving objects subjects them to the possibility of accidents and forms the most serious threat to their long-term stability. This will be considered in some detail in the following sections.

Display cases

Display cases provide a twofold function: protecting the object from the risk of theft and damage, as well as providing a level of protection from the surrounding environment. Although ceramics are relatively resistant to organic vapours, the cases should ideally be constructed from inert materials such as metal and glass. The glass should be laminated rather than toughened – on impact laminated glass shatters and remains in position while toughened glass tends to break and fall apart putting the objects within the case at risk. Shelves, if made of glass, must be strong enough to bear the load with secure fixings that can be adjusted to alter the height of the shelves if desired.

If the display case is required to act as a barrier to the external environment, it should be as airtight as possible. The case should also seek to minimise vibration by being securely attached to the floor; however, case construction will probably not reduce vibration caused by external factors. Any lighting should be accessible from the outside of the case and housed in a separate compartment in order that lamps and fittings can be easily maintained without any risk to the objects. Internal lights may cause a build-up of heat inside cases that can affect objects, particularly those that have been restored.

In display cases that also house moisture-sensitive objects, it may be desirable to incorporate passive humidity buffers such as silica gel. Ideally it is preferable if the buffer can be contained in a separate part of the display case so that it can be independently accessed and maintained. However, the time involved in ensuring regular maintenance of the silica gel should be taken into account together with the implications in terms of labour costs.

Storage

For numerous reasons, it is unlikely that a museum's collection of ceramics will be on display in its entirety at any one time; a portion will usually be held in storage. While many objects may remain in storage indefinitely, others may just spend short periods in storage before being put on display. A store should provide safe, secure and environmentally stable conditions for the objects.

In an ideal situation, the store would be located in an area easily accessible from display areas, conservation studios and curators' offices in order to reduce the distances over which objects are carried. However, in many museums, display space is so limited that objects have to be stored in rather remote parts of the building such as basements, or even offsite in another part of the town or city. Often it is necessary to make do with what already exists. Although this may not be ideal, there are ways of improving spaces to make them safer for the objects.

It is important that the store is not overcrowded by cases and objects. The number of objects in the store should relate to the number of storage cases and this in turn will be determined by the amount of space in the store. Just under half the floor space should be occupied by cases. A less expensive alternative to cases is open shelving with polythene sheeting over the front. The floor should be of a non-slip material and of a uniform level with no steps or other potential obstacles. The storage area should be kept free of pollutants by taking care not to introduce potentially contaminating materials such as wood, adhesives and varnishes that might emit organic acids. Ideally, care should also be taken to exclude particulate pollutants and any external gaseous pollutants (such as nitrogen dioxide, sulphur dioxide and hydrogen sulphide). As it is prohibitively expensive to install pollution control devices, dense plantation around the building may help to overcome this problem to some extent, but obviously is not a practical solution where land is at a premium in densely built-up cities.

Storage cases

Storage cases and cupboards should be strong, stable and secure. Like display cases, the ideal materials are metal and glass, preferably with glass doors so that the objects can be observed easily without the need to unlock the case. Wooden cases, although not ideal, are less expensive. If a wide range of objects of various sizes is to be stored together, adjustable shelves will be helpful. The doors should be well sealed to guard against ingress of dust and pollutants.

The risk of physical damage to ceramics makes it important to avoid overcrowding the objects. There should be adequate space to allow access to each individual piece. Stacking flat objects such as tiles, plates or plaques should be avoided as this will introduce stresses and increase the possibility of accidents. There may be instances where space is extremely limited when stacking may be unavoidable; only those objects that are sound and stable should be included. Layers of padding (i.e. tissue or foam) should be used to separate each object. Small objects or tall, thin

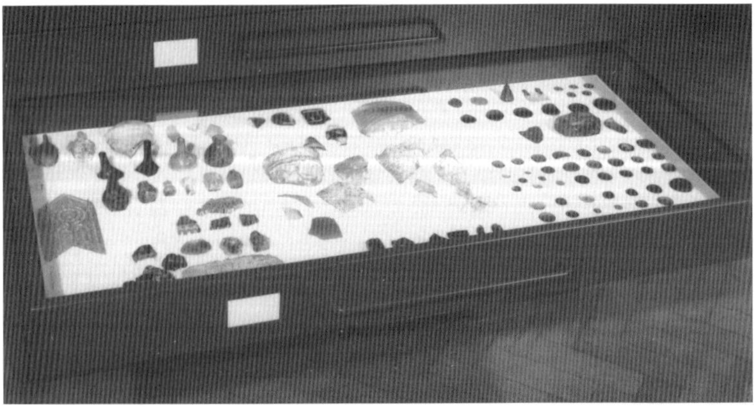

Figure 3.3 A plan chest used for the storage and display of small fragments of varying shapes and sizes.

objects that are potentially unstable should be placed in their most stable position lying down on a nest of foam or tissue to prevent them rolling.

Plan chests may be useful for storing fragmentary objects or tiles; it is important that the objects are properly protected from the effects of the motion of the drawers. This can be achieved through the use of cushioning materials such as heavy density polyethylene foam which can be cut to accommodate the shape of the object. Materials such as cotton wool are best avoided as packing materials because their fibres may snag on rough surfaces (Fig. 3.3).

Care should be taken when lifting objects out of the storage cases especially if they are unavoidably crowded. Obstructing objects should be moved out of the case or to one side rather than attempt to lift one object over another. An object should not be dragged over the shelf, particularly if it is heavy, as it may scratch and abrade the base as well as causing vibration on the shelf. Each case and shelf should be numbered so that it is possible to assign a location to each object, which should be recorded within the collection's system.

Objects too big to be placed inside a case may have to be left in the open in the store. They can be placed on pallets to make them easier to move and covered with acid-free tissue, polythene or Tyvek® (a super-bonded olefin material which is inert, gas permeable and non-abrasive).

Precautions during handling

As already stated, one of the main risks of damage to ceramics is, without doubt, human intervention. Ideally ceramics should never be moved, since any movement will involve handling in order to transfer the objects from one situation to another and this immediately introduces an element of risk from physical damage. It would, of course, be unreasonable to think that we can keep ceramics permanently under lock and key in display and storage cases indefinitely: objects need to be accessible for the purposes of research, study, loans and exhibitions. The potential risk of any damage occurring may be reduced by preparing and evaluating the situation.

Initial considerations

However small the distance, it is a wise precaution to plan and prepare before moving an object. The following points are worth considering:

- Check that personal effects such as loose clothing or jewellery will not be a hazard. Rings, bracelets, watches and long necklaces should be removed as they may catch or chip delicate ceramics and long hair or ties should be kept out of the way to avoid them snagging on objects. Wearing flat, comfortable shoes with non-slip soles should prevent any risk of slipping or tripping on polished or uneven surfaces.
- The route should be checked to ensure that it is free of obstacles such as furniture, cables or barriers. It is important to check that doorways are wide enough, that any steps are easily negotiable and that the route is well lit. The destination location should also be checked to confirm that it is suitably prepared to receive objects.
- A ladder should be used when accessing objects housed on high shelves. In such a situation a second person will be required to whom the object can be passed.
- By far the safest approach is to use a strong container such as a basket, deep-sided tray or box in order to transport the object. The container can be padded with wads of acid-free tissue, polyethylene foam or other suitable material that will provide cushioning. Never use newspaper as packing or wrapping material as the ink is transferred very easily onto hands and also ceramics.

Preparation

- An examination of the object should be made prior to handling. Damage such as cracks, old breaks, weak areas and unstable surfaces will demand a very careful approach to handling.
- Objects with separate moveable parts such as lids or stands should be moved one part at a time.
- Some particularly large or heavy objects may require more than one person to lift them. It is important to plan the operation so that the lifting operation is performed in unison.

Handling

- The cardinal rule should be to keep handling to a minimum.
- Hands should be clean and dry. Disposable vinyl or nitrile gloves should be worn when handling ceramics with surfaces that might mark easily. Unglazed wares will readily take up grease or sweat from hands.
- Both hands should be used and only one object should be lifted at a time (Fig. 3.4).

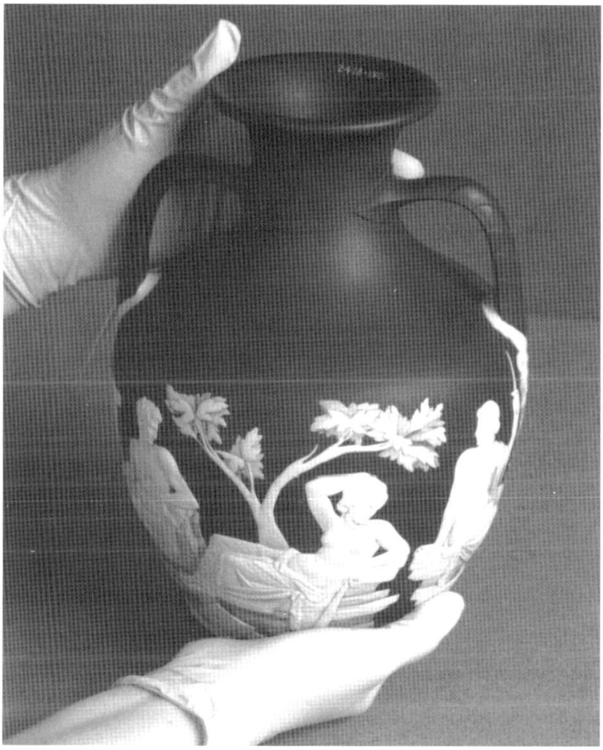

Figure 3.4 A vase should be lifted with both hands. One hand bears most of the weight of the object below its centre of gravity, while the other supports and protects the upper part.

- It is important to concentrate fully on the task and not to be distracted, as this is the time when accidents are most likely to occur. The process of lifting the object should be carried out calmly and slowly.
- When moving objects out of a cupboard or case, the path should be made clear by moving other objects out of the way to make room. Ensure that the top of the object does not hit the shelf above or the top of the case.
- The object should always be held directly below its centre of gravity, supported with one hand underneath the object, while shielded and steadied with the other hand.
- An object should only be handled by its strongest parts. The weakest and most vulnerable areas of ceramics tend to be the extended parts such as the finials, spouts, knops and limbs. If these have been damaged or restored in the past they are likely to be the weakest parts.

Similarly, even if the object has a handle, it is good practice to avoid using it to pick up the object as it may be weak or may have been restored.

- Under no circumstances should one object be lifted over another.
- It is important when lifting heavy objects to keep the back straight, using the legs and arms as leverage. The load should be distributed as evenly as possible. If the object is too large or heavy more than one person may be required to lift it; in certain situations slings or hoists may be appropriate.

Transferring objects over short distances

If the object is being moved within the building from one room to another, a box or basket can be used in which to place it. This is much safer than carrying the object in the hands, as the box, when padded, will provide good protection and be much easier to carry.

- Each object should be clearly visible within the container. Small objects such as lids can be cradled within a single tissue wad. Very small objects such as beads or fragments should be packed in a tray within the basket, taking care to count each object into the tray and then out again at the other end. Small, white objects should be tagged so that they are clearly visible in the tissue.
- Each object should be spaced so that it does not touch any other. Wads of acid-free tissue can be used as padding, packed firmly around robust objects to protect them from movement but more lightly around fragile objects (Fig. 3.5).
- The centre of gravity within the basket must be kept central and low. It is preferable not to pack objects of greatly dissimilar weight. All objects should be placed on their sides if possible.
- No part of an object should be allowed to overhang the sides of the container where it might catch or knock against something.
- The container must be kept level at all times. If two people are sharing the load, it is best for them to hold an end each and to walk side by side with the container in between. When walking up or down stairs, it is even more important that the container be kept level; each person will have to adjust their holding position in order to compensate for the difference in height between the person in front and the one behind. The basket should be held steady avoiding any rocking or swinging motion.

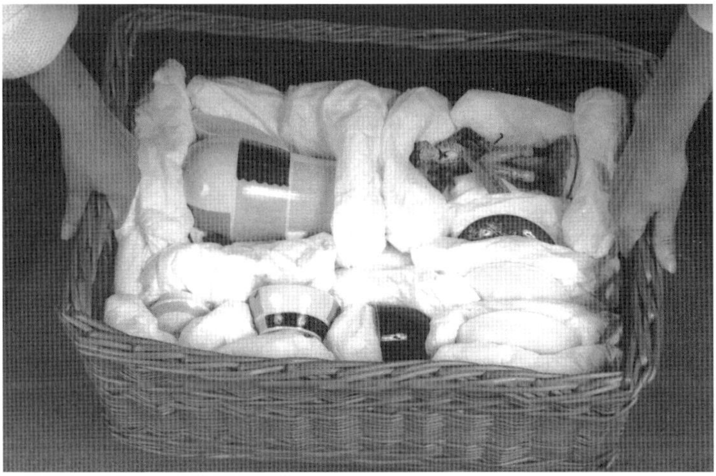

Figure 3.5 A basket packed with tissue wads can be safely used to transfer objects over short distances.

- When passing through closed or locked doors, the basket should be placed on the floor while the door is opened and restrained with door jams or wall hooks. The basket is then carried through the door and placed out of the way while the door is shut.

Packing for transportation

When transporting ceramics over longer journeys, it will be necessary to provide maximum protection for the objects against the risk of any damage. The level of protection and its degree of sophistication will, to a certain extent, be determined by the mode of transport and the distance over which the object will have to travel. For longer journeys, where several different methods of transport are involved, the risks will be greater. In order to guard against the unknown, the protection provided by the packing will need to be correspondingly greater.

On journeys where the risk may be considered smaller – for example when travelling a short distance by road – the packing technique can be relatively simple yet fully effective. Strong cardboard boxes, although not ideal, can be used provided they are in good condition. The box should be well padded with foam, wads of tissue or other appropriate cushioning materials.

Objects should be individually wrapped with inert packing materials such as acid-free tissue. As previously stated, old newspapers should never be used, nor should cotton wool unless it is isolated from the objects to prevent fibres snagging on delicate parts. It is important to plan the packing in advance with the aim of distributing the various objects within the packing so that the heavier items are placed at the bottom and the smaller, lighter ones near the top – separated by abundant padding between layers.

For longer journeys involving road, rail, sea or air, the packing method will need to be very carefully considered. If possible, assistance from a specialist fine art packer should be sought. Containers will need to be robust and ideally made of wood or metal. The internal linings and packing will have to provide adequate protection against vibration, shock and rapid changes or extremes of temperature. Foams are now available in a range of different densities and should be selected to provide appropriate cushioning and shock absorbency for the job. The preferred method of packing in such instances is to cut contoured spaces out of the foam to accommodate the shape of the object which is wrapped in acid-free tissue. Clearly this is a costly approach as the foam can rarely be reused once cut. It is possible to achieve comparable protection using other packing methods, such as carefully prepared tissue wads, although obviously this approach requires experience and skill to obtain optimum results. Materials such as polystyrene peanuts or shredded paper should not be used as they offer little restraint for heavy items, which will gradually settle to the bottom of the container.

Clear instructions for unpacking the container, together with any photographs or diagrams, should be placed on the uppermost layer of packing within the container. An identifying label should be added to the outside taking care to consider the security of the objects and avoid revealing specific information about the nature of the contents.

CHAPTER FOUR

Examination and documentation

The earlier sections have emphasised that ceramic objects are relatively stable if cared for properly. However, their physical properties are such that irreversible damage is not uncommon and as a consequence many objects are likely to have been repaired to some extent in the past. A major part of the work of the ceramics conservators is therefore concerned with de-restoration and re-restoration of objects. The processes involved in the conservation of an object can be divided into a series of distinct stages which will be outlined in the following sections.

Initial considerations

Through their work, conservators are committed to returning the damaged object to a condition that is closely allied to its original strength and appearance. The aim is to lessen the overall impact of the damage in terms of the physical, historical and aesthetic integrity of the object by adopting a sensitive and minimal approach to treatment.

Prior to starting any conservation treatment there are a number of important considerations which the conservator should carefully review:

- The reason for treatment and whether it is strictly necessary.
- The various options for treatment and the level of interaction with the fabric of the object.
- The possibility that a non-interventive approach might be more appropriate or safer.
- Whether s/he has the necessary skills and knowledge to safely carry out the treatment.
- The need to consult other specialists for guidance and advice.

- The existence of any earlier records and documentation.
- The threat to the interpretation of any evidence of a historical, technical or aesthetic nature.
- The durability and reversibility of the materials and techniques to be used and the implications of their use on any future choice of treatment.
- Whether restoration of missing areas is desirable, and if there is appropriate evidence on which to base the reconstruction. Restoration of such areas should be carried out only to the minimum extent necessary and should be thoroughly recorded.
- The full documentation of details of the treatment and the materials used. Such records should be accessible to conservators in the future.

Examination

One of the most crucial stages of the conservation process is the initial examination. The main purpose will be first, to determine the nature and extent of any damage or deterioration, and secondly, to reveal the various characteristics of the ceramic. Only after examination will it be possible to suggest whether conservation is indeed necessary, and, if so, the most appropriate approach (see Appendix 1). Any examination process should always be backed up with detailed documentation.

There are numerous specialist examination techniques available for the examination and analysis of ceramics which will provide further information to assist the conservator in a choice of treatment, as well as determining aspects of the object's technology, date of manufacture and provenance. Although the more sophisticated methods can prove invaluable in furthering research, they are usually beyond the scope of small conservation laboratories for obvious economic reasons. The majority of objects which a ceramics conservator will routinely come across will not require more specialised equipment than the items described in the following section.

Basic examination techniques

- *Visual examination:* this is the first stage in examining any object when it first arrives in the conservation laboratory. Besides observing the nature of any damage in more detail, it will also help reveal the type of body, its texture, density, hardness, porosity and the nature of any decorative surface. These physical characteristics relate to the nature of the ceramic, their initial composition and the conditions during firing and will affect the choice of treatment. Any visual examination must be carried out in good lighting conditions in order to be reliable. Raking light (light directed at the surface at an angle almost parallel to the surface plane) can show up surface irregularities and textures.

- *Auditory examination*: objects in good condition produce a clear resonating tone when gently tapped or knocked with the tip of a finger or a wooden modelling tool. The presence of a flaw such as a hairline crack will cause a dulling of the tone. Similarly, insecure and lifting glazes can sometimes be detected by lightly tapping the surface with a fingernail.
- *Hand-lens*: a simple hand-held magnifier can extend the powers of the human eye up to ten times depending on the individual magnifier. The extent of restorations will be clearer. Areas of exposed body will allow an opportunity to look at the physical characteristics of the ceramic. Various clues about the process of manufacture such as fingerprints and tool marks should be more apparent under low magnification.
- *Optical microscopy*: more detailed examination will be possible with a microscope. These range from simple binocular microscopes that can be used at the bench (Fig. 4.1), through to much more sophisticated instruments with zoom facilities, fibre-optic lighting and attachments for cameras.
- *Metal detector*: a hand-held metal detector, such as those used by electricians to detect concealed cables, can assist in showing up concealed metal components used in old restorations such as dowels.

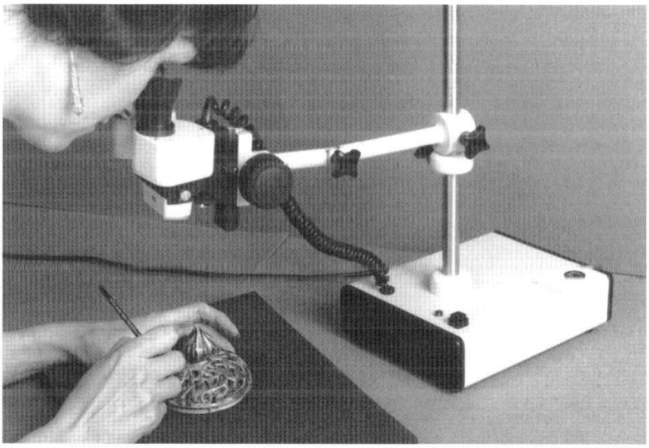

Figure 4.1 A binocular microscope.

- *Ultraviolet (UV) light*: provided by a hand-held lamp, UV light can be used to examine the surface of a ceramic object. In darkened conditions it may be possible to detect areas of restoration where synthetic resins have been used to fill or retouch the object. Eyes should be protected with appropriate glasses to avoid exposure to the harmful effects of UV light.

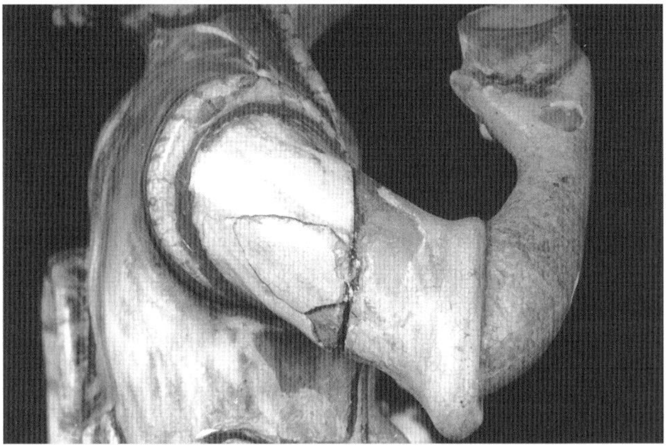

Figure 4.2 Old repair of the arm of a majolica figure which forms the subject of the X-ray in Figure 4.3.

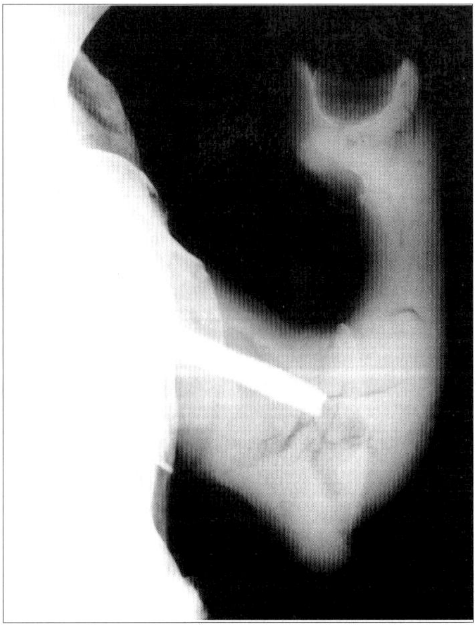

Figure 4.3 A metal dowel is revealed concealed within the arm by the X-ray.

- *Infrared photography*: infrared photography is sometimes used for examination of indistinct surfaces that have been obscured by overlying material. Unfired materials such as traces of paint and ink may become visible.
- *X-radiography*: although beyond the scope of smaller laboratories, X-radiography can be useful in the examination of objects showing up metal components such as dowels or armatures. Air spaces, stress points and inclusions may be visible and help in interpreting fabrication techniques. It should be remembered that the use of X-rays for examination of an object may affect or invalidate results that may be obtained if the object is to be dated by thermo-luminescence (Figs 4.2 and 4.3).

Recording and documentation

Although examination is usually considered the first stage in the series of events involved in conserving an object, the process of recording and documenting observations and actions should, in theory, be commenced at around the same time. The primary purpose of making records is to ensure that the information involved in the processes of conservation is not forgotten or permanently lost. Such information can be valuable if it becomes necessary to monitor the condition of an object or to re-treat it later. In the case of excavated ceramics, certain details may also be relevant for the archaeological record.

Although the future of documentation, for larger organisations, lies with information technology and computerisation, such an approach will continue to be inappropriate and out of reach for smaller conservation laboratories. While notebooks can be used by the conservator for jotting down brief observations, reminders and drawings, a standard form or card allows a more systematic approach. Such record cards are usually best designed by the users. In order to extend their lifespan such cards should be made of archival quality paper and inks, particularly in hot and humid climates, and filled in by the conservator with a permanent pen of archival quality. The format should include a section for standard information that describes, identifies and locates the object (e.g., museum number, location, type, manufacturer, date, materials, and techniques). There should also be a section to describe the object's condition prior to conservation. The main part of the card will be taken up by the description of the treatment process and should include information about the techniques and the materials used, giving both the proprietary name and chemical name (Fig. 4.4).

V&A CERAMICS & GLASS CONSERVATION **TREATMENT RECORD CARD**

MUSEUM NO: IS. 48 – 1898

MUSEUM NO.	COLLECTION	CONSERVATOR
IS.48-1898	Indian Department	A. Rees

OBJECT	MATERIALS & TECHNIQUES
Ceramic Tile	Glazed earthenware
ARTIST / DESIGNER / MAKER: Unknown	
ORIGIN / FACTORY: Lahore, India.	PROJECT TITLE: Exhibition: Tiles of Asia

PERIOD / DATE	MATERIAL RETAINED IN FILE ? [ ]	RISK ASSESSMENT COMPLETED ? [✓]
17th Century		

DATE RECEIVED	DATE STARTED	DATE FINISHED	TIME SPENT
20.03.99	02.04.99	18.04.99	5 HRS 1/2 MINS

CONDITION

Surface disfigured by ingrained and superficial dirt. Residues of black paint visible on surface and at edges. Glaze very scratched and abraded with areas of intense wear; several areas of loss. Edges of tile worn and irregular. Three metal loops set in plaster in drilled holes on reverse. Edges worn and irregular.

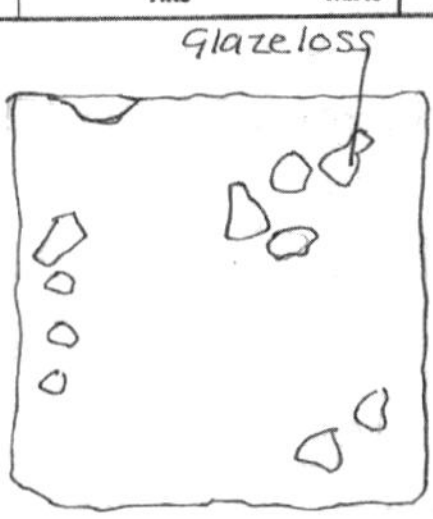

TREATMENT	PHOTOGRAPHIC / ANALYTICAL DOCUMENTATION
1. Cleaned with warm water and SYNPERONIC N (non-ionic detergent). Rinsed in deionised water. Paint removed mechanically with scalpel viewed under magnification. 2. Areas of body exposed by glaze loss consolidated with PARALOID B-72 (ethyl methacrylate methyl acrylate copolymer) 5% w/v in acetone. 3. Losses filled with FINE SURFACE POLYFILLA (vinyl acetate copolymer with inorganic mineral fillers. 4. Retouched with GOLDEN ACRYLIC VARNISH mixed with dry artists pigments. 5. Metal loops removed with wire clippers.	2 views front + reverse (35mm colour transparencies) Before treat and after.

(PTO)

Figure 4.4 Example of a treatment record card used to document the condition and treatment of the object.

While drawings may also help to give more information, photography has the potential to provide a more accurate result. Ideally several photos should be taken: before, during and after treatment. The choice of whether to use black and white, colour or digital photography is largely determined by personal preference, cost or organisational policy. Polaroid photographs should be avoided as they deteriorate rapidly and are unsuitable as archival records.

When working on site at an archaeological excavation, any first-aid or emergency treatment should be accurately documented. The work that follows later at the conservation laboratory can then be carried out with a clear understanding of the cleaning or stabilisation processes that have gone before.

CHAPTER FIVE

Removal of previous restoration materials

After the initial examination of a ceramic object, the removal of previous restoration materials is often the next stage in the conservation process. The removal of old repairs may be necessary for various reasons. The properties of the materials used in the past are such that they do not always withstand the test of time. This may become apparent in a number of ways: a change in colour, shrinkage, loss of mechanical properties, embrittlement and cross-linkage. In other instances the repairs may have been applied in such a way that they are unsightly, misleading and unsafe.

The safety and historic integrity of the object should always be paramount when deciding on the best course of action. It is not always necessary to dismantle and remove old repairs – the risks involved to the object should be carefully considered. Old repairs may have some intrinsic interest or aesthetic value; they may also be interesting in the context of the history of restoration techniques. If a process is not strictly necessary and can be avoided, this may be the best and safest course of action. In some instances it may be possible to upgrade the existing repair without having to undertake the full conservation treatment, an approach that is obviously preferable.

Surface coatings

Old paint and coatings can be removed using mechanical methods or through the use of solvents. The mechanical approach involves the controlled use of a sharp scalpel. Extreme care must be taken when using this method in order to avoid scratching or damaging the underlying surface, and for this reason is best carried out with the aid of a binocular microscope. On unglazed surfaces, it may be necessary to remove the surface coating with solvents. Tests should always be performed first with a range of solvents applied on cotton wool swabs, starting with those least harmful to the health of the user: water, then industrial methylated spirits (IMS), or ethanol, followed by acetone. Particular attention should be paid to any unfired decoration that might be affected by the solvent. Water contact should be avoided with very low or unfired pottery, unfired decoration or pottery contaminated by salts.

Application of the solvent is through use of cotton wool swabs on swab-sticks, gently rolling the swab over the surface. In some instances, it may be necessary to use a stronger solvent in the form of a paint-stripper (e.g., Nitromors). These are generally available in a water-washable gel form. They are painted onto the surface and left until the coating has bubbled up. The use of toxic solvents, such as dichloromethane, must be carried out in a well-ventilated area or using personal protective equipment to avoid inhalation; the skin should also be protected from contact.

Adhesives

Solvents are commonly used for separating joins. Mechanical methods are generally only appropriate for removing remaining adhesive residues once the object has been taken apart. The choice of solvent is determined by identifying the resin (Table 5.1). Any previous documentation will assist this process, otherwise it will be necessary to resort to observations of visual, physical and chemical properties.

The solvent is applied to the adhesive in the form of a vapour, liquid or gel. It may be possible to enclose the object in a sealed container with a small amount of the solvent which evaporates, creating an atmosphere within the container that gradually breaks down the adhesive. Alternatively the solvent may be applied in swabs of cotton wool or blotting paper, which are left in place over the joins. Solvents can be mixed into gels such as carboxymethyl cellulose. Evaporation of the solvent may be controlled through the use of polythene sheeting.

Precautions

- Low-fired or unfired ceramics will be particularly vulnerable to such treatments and spot tests are recommended.
- Any gilding or unfired decoration should be tested prior to continuing with the chosen treatment.

- It may be necessary to give additional support to large objects during dismantling to avoid sudden uncontrolled collapse.
- When selecting a solvent, it is advisable to choose the least toxic first.

Table 5.1 Identification and methods of removing adhesives

Adhesive	Appearance	Methods for removal
Animal glue	Pale yellow to brown.	Soluble in warm water.
Shellac	Light red to dark brown (hard and brittle with age).	Usually very difficult to remove, • a 50/50 mix of ethyl alcohol and acetone may swell the adhesive allowing the join to be released • apply paint strippers containing dichloromethane (toxic and suspected carcinogen) • immerse object in pyridine and place in a sealed container in a fume cupboard (toxic and highly flammable) • as a last resort, heated industrial methylated spirits (or ethanol) may assist in the removal of shellac, but extreme care should be exercised when warming the IMS as it is highly flammable. A violet stain frequently results.
Cellulose nitrate	Water white to yellow (depending on age).	Soluble in acetone, use acetone vapour in a sealed container.
Rubber adhesives	Yellow to brown with elastic consistency.	May be possible to peel it away. Dichloromethane will swell the adhesive. The use of a steam cleaner may soften it.
Silicone adhesives	Transparent or milky-white. Tend to be insoluble in most solvents and very difficult to remove.	Attempt mechanical removal with care. May leave oily stains.
Poly(vinyl acetate) emulsion	White, clear or slightly brown, rubbery or brittle, depending on age.	Warm water or acetone may gradually break down the joins. Ethanol and industrial methylated spirits mixed with water may prove effective.
Epoxy resins	Water white, light yellow or brown and very hard.	Insoluble, will soften and swell in dichloromethane or commercially available paint stripper.
Polyester resins	Clear yellow when fresh, ageing to dark orange-brown.	As for epoxy.
Acrylic resins (e.g. Paraloid/ Acryloid B-72)	Water white resin.	Soluble in acetone.
Acrylic resins (e.g. 'Superglue')	White to yellow.	Initially soluble in acetone or in adhesive-specific solvent, but later soften only after extended soaking.
Pressure-sensitive tapes	Sticky residues remain after tape is removed which attract dirt.	Soluble in white spirit while still soft.

Fills

Gap-fills may be weakened during the process of removing the adhesive from the joins allowing them to be eased away, although those fillings not associated with break-lines are likely to stay in place. Old fillings may be made of plaster-based compounds or synthetic resins, sometimes with dowels or armatures concealed inside them. Methods for their removal will be either mechanical or chemical. Plaster fills can be softened with water, although the risk of soluble salts being drawn into the body from the plaster should be considered. Resin fills can be removed by various mechanical means depending on their size and position. Tools such as pins, scalpels, drills and hacksaws may be used.

Rivets

Rivets were often used in the past to hold shards together. There are a number of variations in the technique, which involves inserting metal staples to bridge both sides of the break using pre-drilled pairs of holes to anchor the ends of the staple. The holes were often drilled at an angle towards the break so that the ends of the rivet pointed inwards; any gaps around the rivet were filled with plaster, lead or other fillers (Fig. 5.1). Occasionally the rivets were embellished to enhance them and create a decorative feature. Careful consideration should always be given to the necessity of removing rivets as they can be regarded as part of the object's

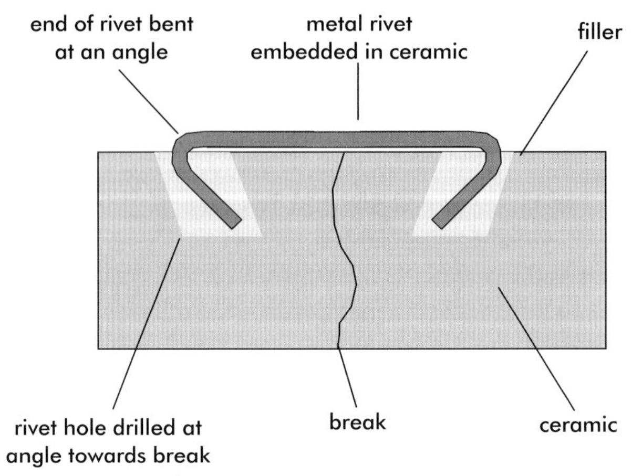

Figure 5.1 Section through a joint which has been repaired with a rivet.

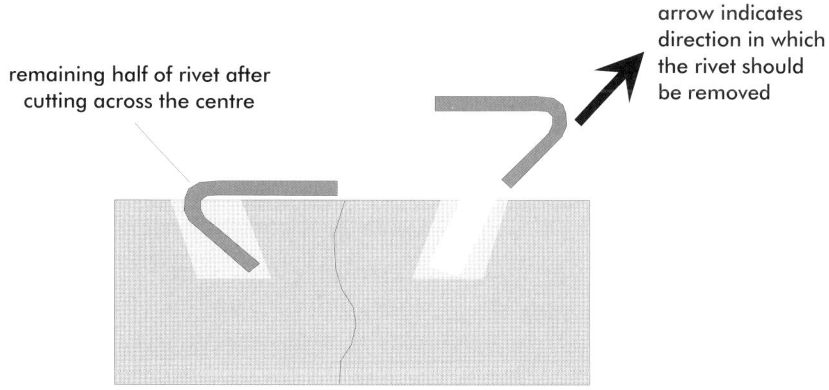

Figure 5.2 The removal of the rivet after cutting across the centre.

history. Provided they are not placing the object at any risk, they may be worth retaining and preserving. If, however, they are unsightly, loose or causing damage such as staining, intervention may be unavoidable.

Safe removal can only be ensured by cutting through the middle of the rivet so that each half can be eased away at the correct angle (Fig. 5.2). This can be achieved by first picking away the filling material around the rivet hole using a scalpel or a needle held in a pin-vice. Provided there is no risk of staining, this stage may be made easier by softening the filler with a swab of cotton wool moistened with water (note that water should not be used if there are corrosion products on the rivet or excess dirt in close proximity that might cause staining). Sometimes it may then be possible to carefully ease the rivet away at this stage, depending on the angle of the ends. More often it is necessary to cut through the rivet with a short length of fine hacksaw blade. The surrounding ceramic should be carefully masked with tape during the process in order to protect the glaze from damage. During removal of the rivets the object should be supported using lengths of adhesive tape to hold the shards together.

Often the conservator will come across variations in the type of rivets. Sometimes they are bound with wire then soldered to hold them in place. Occasionally, instead of rivets, wire would be threaded through pairs of holes, piercing right through the ceramic, lacing the shards together. The ends of the wire would be twisted together, thus tightening the join, and the twisted ends then flattened towards the body. A similar approach to that described above is used for their removal: using a hacksaw to carefully cut the lace and then ease away the two parts.

Dowels

This technique involved the mechanical joining of fragments using a short length of a material such as metal, wood or even bone inserted into holes drilled into the two break edges. Any spaces around the dowel holes would be packed with a filler or adhesive, and once the two parts were united the dowels would be concealed below the surface. Since dowels are hidden within the walls of the ceramic their presence is often difficult to detect. During the course of treatment, if a join resists repeated applications of solvent and does not appear to separate, hidden dowels are likely to be the cause of the problem. X-ray examination would confirm this.

In order to remove dowels, repeated applications of an appropriate solvent may be necessary before the join can be eased apart enough to allow a hacksaw blade to be inserted. After separating, the stumps of the dowel can be removed mechanically or by applying further solvent.

CHAPTER SIX

Approaches to cleaning

The process of cleaning a ceramic object involves the removal of foreign material that is not part of the original fabric. Within this definition we can include superficial dirt and staining caused by use, handling, atmospheric pollutants, burial, fire damage and previous repair materials. The aim of the cleaning process is generally to remove the disfiguration which may be masking the colour, decoration and surface texture. Damage such as cracks, breaks, chips or crazing may also be emphasised by the accumulation of dirt. Except in the case of salts – another form of unwanted material capable of causing more serious damage – dirt itself is likely to cause little damage.

It should be emphasised that removal of dirt can, in some instances, cause damage. Indeed, it is not always desirable or necessary to remove foreign material, particularly if the material is of intrinsic historical or ethnographic interest. On archaeological objects, burial material may contain residues of foods or cremation remains and it would be considered inappropriate to remove such materials. Occasionally foreign material may prove impossible to remove without the risk of damage to the object. In all these instances, it is only through careful examination and discussion with curators and archaeologists that the most appropriate course of action can be identified. It therefore follows that a clear understanding of the nature of the object and its condition is vital when selecting an appropriate method for cleaning.

The processes for removing dirt vary according to whether it is restricted to the surface of the object or whether it has become absorbed into the body. If at all uncertain when dealing with unfamiliar materials or problems, it is advisable to carry out tests on a small unobtrusive area of the object in order to confirm that there is no risk of damage. Testing is also particularly important when dealing with any unfired decoration. In general, much greater caution should be observed with removal of dirt from low-fired wares due to their high porosity and tendency to readily absorb liquids. The low porosity of high-fired wares such as stoneware and porcelain makes them much less vulnerable to such damage.

Surface dirt

The removal of surface dirt from low-fired porous wares will prevent the potential problem of the dirt being absorbed into the body or pushed into surface flaws. There are two main approaches to the removal of surface dirt: mechanical and chemical. Mechanical methods involve brushing, picking and cutting processes which are relatively easily controlled (depending on the skill of the conservator). Chemical methods involve the use of solvents to dissolve the dirt so that it can then be easily removed in solution; this carries the risk of the dissolved dirt being drawn into the body causing a stain.

Mechanical methods

- *Dusting and brushing* are appropriate methods for dealing with loose dust that has settled on the surface of the object. Dust can be gently pushed away (ideally towards a vacuum cleaner) using a soft brush, cloth or dry cotton wool. The metal ferrules on brushes should be bound with a softer material such as masking tape, fabric or leather to avoid scratching or chipping the object. Areas of unstable or flaking glaze should be avoided. Dry cotton wool or cloths should not be used on unglazed or rough surfaces as fibres may catch or snag on them (Fig. 6.1).
- *Picking and cutting methods* are employed to carefully remove dirt that is more closely attached to the surface of the object. Pins, sewing needles, scalpels, wooden picks and custom-made or modified tools can be used. Again the main risks come from the use of excessive force resulting in scratches to the surface. For maximum control the process should be carried out using a microscope.
- *Abrading* includes a number of cleaning techniques: polishing creams, designed to polish metals and plastics (e.g., Solvol Autochrome and Greygate Plastic Polish), usually consist of a very mild abrasive powder suspended in a liquid or a gel. Household scouring creams should not be used as they are too aggressive. The polishing creams can be used on glazed surfaces to lift dirt from small scratches and pits. To apply, the tip of a swab-stick, wrapped in cotton wool, should

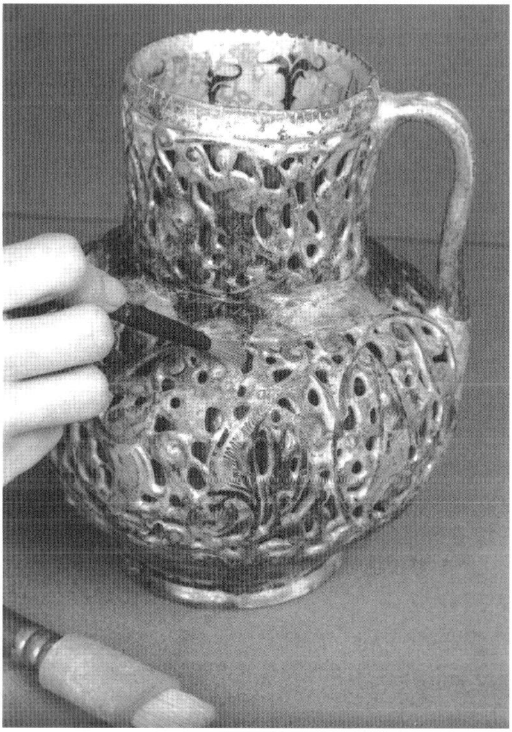

Figure 6.1 The delicate surface of an object is gently cleaned with a sable brush. The metal parts of the brush have been bound with tape to prevent any scratching.

be dipped into the cream and then worked over the surface in a circular motion. Residues can be removed with white spirit. The use of abrasive materials has to be carefully controlled and should not be used where there is any unfired decoration, gilding or instability of the surface.

- *Rubberised materials* such as plastic erasers, rubber powders (e.g., Draft Clean) can be very effective at removing surface dirt from unglazed rough surfaces. Similarly, putty rubbers can also be quite useful. Some rubberised materials may leave residues behind and for this reason tests should always be carried out.

Aqueous and chemical methods

- *Water* is is the safest, cheapest and most effective solvent for removing dirt. Water contact should be avoided on certain groups of objects including: those with old restorations, cracks, chips, breaks, flaking glaze, unstable decoration, salt contamination, a low or unfired body, cold-painted decoration or metal mounts. High-fired non-porous wares such as stoneware and porcelain can be safely immersed in water contained in a plastic bowl to which a few drops of an appropriate detergent have been added, and then cleaned with a small soft brush or pad of cotton wool. Washing must then be followed by thorough rinsing in clean, or preferably deionised or distilled water. After washing the object should be dried with paper towels. Low-fired wares should not be submerged in water as there is a greater risk of damage by staining, but they can be cleaned using damp swabs of cotton wool which should be rolled (rather than dragged) across the surface on swab sticks (Fig. 6.2). When cleaning unglazed pottery, great care should be taken never to allow prolonged water contact.

Painted decoration or gilding on all types of ceramic should always be spot-tested before cleaning to determine its fastness. An inconspicuous area should be carefully dabbed with a swab of damp cotton wool, checking the swab for any particles of decoration.

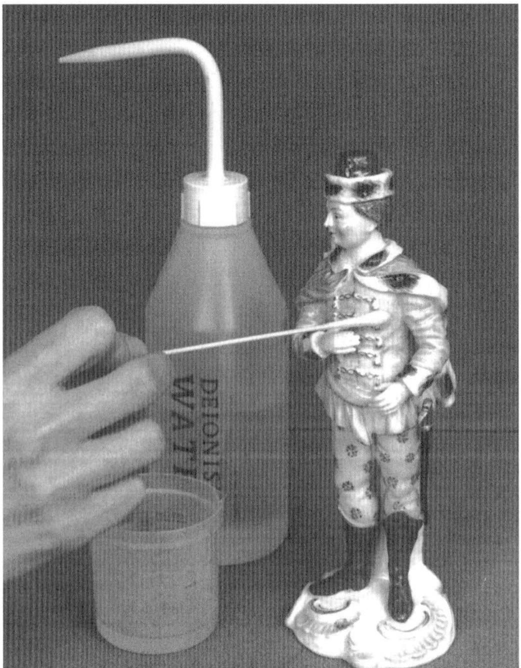

Figure 6.2 A figurine is cleaned with a cotton wool swab that has been moistened with deionised water.

An alternative method to the use of water is to employ a portable steam cleaning unit to remove dirt from an object. The steam cleaner should be appropriate for the application with a fine nozzle emitting a jet of steam that can be controlled by varying the pressure. The finely focused jet of hot steam can be focused on areas of ingrained dirt such as cracks and pits. Textured and unglazed surfaces can also be effectively cleaned. As the steam comes into contact with the surface, the dirt is immediately blotted away with paper towels, thus quickly lifting away the dirt and avoiding undue wetting. As mentioned earlier for treatments using water, steam cleaning should only be used on sound and stable objects, not on vulnerable low-fired wares except at very low pressures.

- *Solvents* are sometimes used in instances where water has proved ineffective. Again, spot tests are advisable before proceeding with more extensive application. Acetone or industrial methylated spirits (IMS) can be used to degrease the surface. Acetone may be also be used to remove paint and sometimes adhesive residues. White spirit usually proves an effective solvent for greasy residues. A mixture of water and IMS or acetone may be used to improve the evaporation rate of water and avoid over-wetting. The cleaning of low-fired pottery is sometimes carried out using a 50:50 mixture of IMS and water. A 50:50 mixture of white spirit and water and a teaspoon of detergent (to make 600 ml) can be a useful cleaning emulsion for removing stubborn greasy dirt from intact glazed surfaces.
- *Enzymes* can occasionally be used to effectively digest unwanted dirt, allowing it to be rinsed away. Fats, carbohydrates and proteins can be removed using an appropriate type of enzyme (lipase, amylase and protease respectively). There are health and safety issues associated with the handling and use of these substances. Health and safety data sheets and instructions should be carefully followed. One of the components of human saliva is the enzyme amylase, which will assist in removal of certain types of dirt. So-called biological washing powders also contain various enzymes that are designed to break down the various proteins and fats that constitute the dirt found on clothing. In addition to enzymes, such biological washing powders are known to contain numerous other ingredients such as perfumes, optical brighteners and chelating agents, which are not necessary or desirable for cleaning ceramics. The solutions made from the powders are generally reserved for use on high-fired porcelain where there is no risk of absorption into the body. Particularly effective results are achieved in the cleaning of Parian ware or biscuit porcelain. Due to the risk of leaving potentially active ingredients in the body, any

cleaning processes involving the use of biological washing powders should always be followed up with thorough rinsing and soaking in deionised or distilled water for at least 24 hours depending on the porosity of the body.

- *Acids* are occasionally used for the removal of salt encrustations from the surface of objects recovered from archaeological sites, including marine and fresh-water excavations. Such encrustations are generally insoluble carbonates, sulphates or silicates of calcium, and the acids most commonly used include nitric, hydrochloric, acetic, citric and oxalic acids. The processes used in removing such deposits can be dangerous for both the conservator and the object, and should only be performed by experienced conservators or under expert supervision. The main risks to human beings when using any type of acid are permanent tissue damage caused by acid burns. Calcium compounds within the ceramic body, such as chalk or ground shells, may be attacked by acid contact. Also, objects containing iron constituents in their bodies or glazes will be vulnerable to attack by hydrochloric and oxalic acids which can dissolve iron constituents. Similarly, ancient lead glazes on pottery will be vulnerable to acid attack. The object must be pre-soaked in deionised or distilled water and then treated with a solution of the acid, either by localised application or by immersion in the acid. The concentration of the acid will vary depending on the type of acid and the nature of the problem. Treatment is followed by very thorough rinsing.
- *Sequestering agents* (e.g., sodium citrate, trisodium phosphate and the disodium salt of ethylene diamino-tetra-acetic-acid (EDTA)) have occasionally been used in solution to remove surface concretions and dirt. They work by attacking the metal ions in the concretion, combining with them to form complexes that can be rinsed away. There is the obvious risk that the underlying ceramic material may also be attacked, and any metal ions in the body or glaze (such as lustre) may be removed. Because of the dangers of causing irreversible damage, it is stressed that such chemicals must be prepared following proper procedures, using appropriate concentrations and applied under controlled conditions by experienced conservators.
- Lasers, although not fully investigated for the cleaning of ceramics, have been successfully used to remove black encrustations from stone sculptures. The most commonly used type of laser in conservation is the Q-switched Nd:YAG laser. The laser produces pulses of energy as a very intense monochromatic (single colour) beam which is focused on unwanted material. Energy is absorbed leading to rapid heating of the dirt particles and causing them to expand with such force that

they are ejected from the surface. The cleaning can be directed at a precise area and the effect is immediate.

Stain removal

All porous ceramics are vulnerable to the risk of staining, particularly if the body is exposed either by lack of glaze or by damage and flaws to the glaze. Foreign material can be absorbed into the body to become deeply lodged within the pores. Removal is made more complex by the intimate association of the dirt with the ceramic and is not without risk to the object. Many stains are of organic origin having been caused by use and contact with food. It may not always be desirable to remove stains as they may contain important information relating to the use of the object.

Poulticing methods

Stains trapped within the pores of the body can, in theory, be removed again by mobilising the dirt with the help of a solvent. The solvent together with the dirt can be drawn out into a poultice or a pack. Evaporation of the solvent at the surface of the poultice leaves the dirt remaining in the poultice rather than the body. Depending on the nature of the stain, water is commonly used as the solvent. The object is pre-soaked in order to saturate the body and dissolve the stain. The poultice is then applied to the surface of the object. Total coverage is appropriate where the glaze is interrupted by crazing and flaws such as chips, pits and unglazed parts. On objects where the glaze is more or less intact, application can be restricted solely to the areas of the surface where the glaze is absent or where a slight flaw occurs (Fig. 6.3).

There are various poulticing materials available ranging from paper pulp to forms of clay. A paper pulp poultice can be prepared by using ready-made powdered paper (e.g., Arbocel which is obtained as pure cellulose fibre from vegetable origin) or by tearing acid-free blotting paper into small pieces and mixing it with the solvent, usually deionised water, in a beaker to obtain a paste-like consistency. Laponite RD is a synthetic, inorganic fine clay which, when mixed with water (5% by weight), will gradually thicken after 2 hours to form a transparent gel. The gel is then applied to the object to a thickness of 5 mm. Evaporation of the solvent can be controlled by covering the object with polythene. The Laponite RD should be removed before it becomes too hard otherwise it may cause

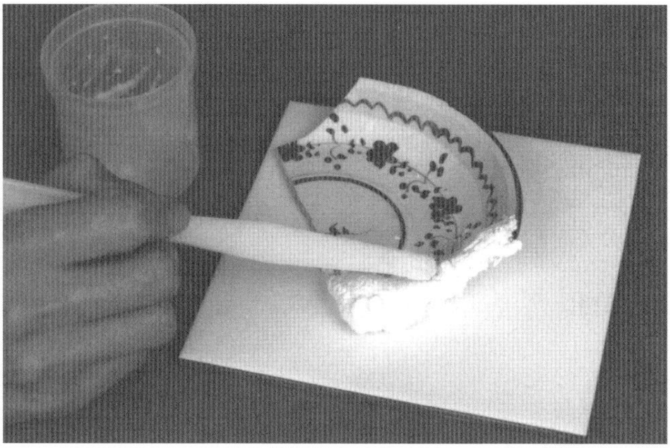

Figure 6.3 The application of a paper poultice to the edge of a stained fragment.

damage. This tendency of Laponite to adhere to the ceramic surface may be reduced by applying a layer of Japanese tissue between the ceramic or by mixing it with Arbocel to modify the absorbency of the poultice. Sepiolite, another poulticing material, is a fine, grey, naturally occurring clay containing hydrated magnesium silicate. The powder is mixed with water to form a paste which is applied to the surface of the object up to a thickness of 2 cm. As the poultice dries, cracks will appear, and after 2–3 days (depending on the prevailing environmental conditions, and whether polythene has been used) the Sepiolite will still be slightly damp and ready to brush away. A dust mask should be worn to provide protection from the small dust particles. All remaining particles of the poulticing material should be removed as far as possible, although total removal of any remaining residues may be harder to ensure.

Bleaches

If the stain cannot be removed it may be possible to render the staining material colourless by using hydrogen peroxide. Inaccessible cracks and break edges can also be successfully cleaned. During the reaction, hydrogen peroxide breaks down to form water and active oxygen which oxidises the organic residues causing removal of the colour. Household domestic bleaches should never be used as they can introduce chlorides into the body, which may prove difficult to remove later.

A 20 volume solution (i.e. a 6% solution) of hydrogen peroxide with a few drops of ammonia can be applied to the object on swabs of cotton wool (Fig.

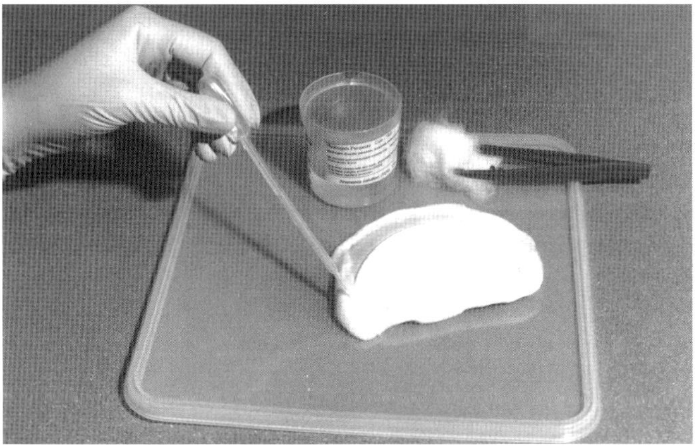

Figure 6.4 The application of hydrogen peroxide to the stained edges of a porcelain object.

6.4). The ammonia serves as a catalyst and speeds up the reaction. The swabs are left in position on the object (which has been previously soaked in water) and checked periodically. Repeated applications with fresh hydrogen peroxide and ammonia can be made if necessary; the solution will remain active for several hours before gradually losing its strength. The treatment should be followed by thorough soaking in deionised water to remove any remaining residues. Hydrogen peroxide is usually reserved for use on non-porous bodies and should be used with great caution on porous ceramics due to the potential risk of components within the ceramic body being adversely affected causing secondary stains. It is always advisable, if possible, to perform a test on a small inconspicuous area, particularly if there are areas of potentially vulnerable gilding or other unusual surface treatments. There is also a risk that residual traces of hydrogen peroxide trapped in the pores of low-fired ceramics may affect subsequent treatments. Precautions should be taken when using hydrogen peroxide to protect the eyes, skin and clothing from the corrosive effects of accidental splashes.

Stains caused by metals

Corrosion of metals in contact with ceramics may give rise to staining. Most commonly the stains originate from iron and copper dowels and rivets. Treatments for the removal of iron stains generally involve the use of an acid (e.g., phosphoric and oxalic acids) and is followed by thorough rinsing. As mentioned earlier, acids should be used with extreme caution due to the risks of potential adverse reactions when used inappropriately.

It is emphasised that such treatments should only be performed under the instruction and guidance of an experienced ceramics conservator. Ammonia can be used to remove copper stains: the solution is applied on swabs, and the treatment followed by thorough washing as before. Other methods of treatment involve the use of bleaches and sequestering agents.

Removal of soluble salts

Salts may be present in porous ceramics for various reasons related to the previous use or environment of the object. When a damp object containing salts dries, salt crystals form which are trapped within the pores of the body. The process of crystallisation will bring about the disruption of the fabric of the body and loss of glaze. The salt crystals occupy a greater volume of space than when the salt is in solution and this places the body of the ceramic under enormous pressure.

It is safer to store freshly excavated pottery, which is known to be contaminated with salts, in an environment similar to that from which it was excavated. Damp storage can lead to stagnant water and mould growth, however the risk can be minimised by storing in low temperatures. When ceramics containing soluble salts have been allowed to dry, the salts will usually appear as fine needle-like crystals on any exposed body. In some instances they may appear as fine powdery deposits. Occasionally it may be necessary to view the surface of the object under magnification in order to see the suspected salts. However, if the object is still damp, the salts of course will not be visible. Tests for identification of the commonly occurring salts – chlorides, nitrates and sulphates – are given in Appendix 2.

Salts are usually removed by allowing them to diffuse into water by various methods (Fig. 6.5). The object should be carefully examined prior to any treatment to confirm that it will be able to withstand treatment without any damage. Very low-fired ware will be at risk, as will unfired decoration. Deteriorated unstable glaze and body may require some initial consolidation in order to prevent any loss or damage. In some instances consolidation may be the preliminary stage. Temporary reinforcement may be necessary to hold any fragments in position and prevent loss while desalination is carried out. Netting or fine Japanese tissue impregnated with resin may be used temporarily to hold fragments together and prevent loss during desalination. Later, the reinforcement can be carefully removed and permanent consolidation then carried out.

As crystallisation and hydration occur at specific RHs, it may be safer to brush off any salt crystals and to store the object in stable environmental

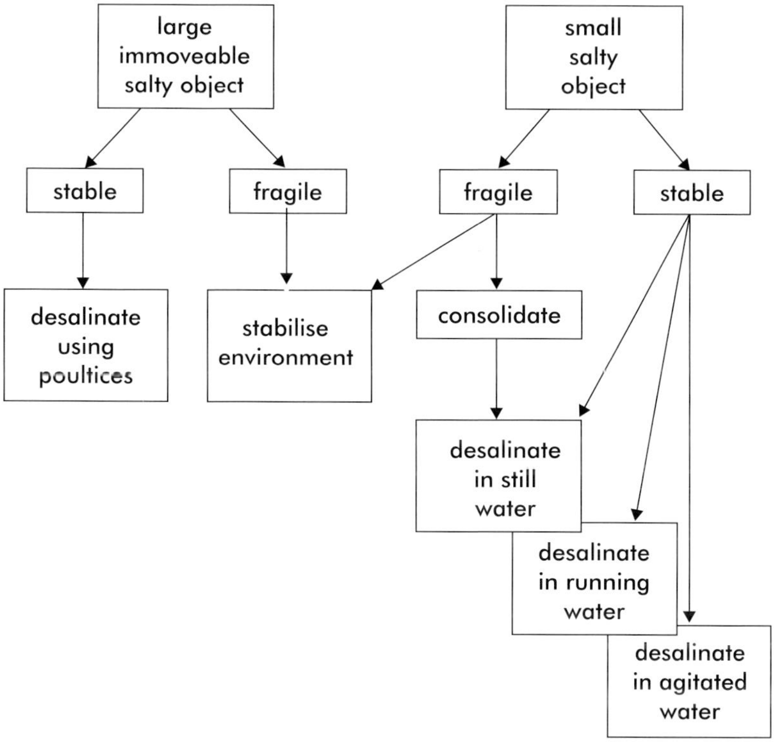

Figure 6.5 Options for removal of soluble salts.

conditions maintaining the ambient RH above or below the critical value. However, the situation is made more complex where mixtures of salts occur.

- *Soaking in static water*: if the object is in sound stable condition it can be placed in a container into which tap water may be slowly poured. Sudden immersion of the dry object into the water should be avoided as the pressure of the air escaping from the pores may cause damage. The object is then left to soak so that the salts can diffuse out into the surrounding water. The water can be changed at regular intervals (approximately between 12 and 24 hours) in order to maintain a differential between the salt concentration in the object and the surrounding water. The salt content of the water is monitored by taking readings with a conductivity meter. When readings start to stabilise, the process can be stopped. For most dissolved salts, 150 micro-siemens per cubic centimetre is considered acceptable; obviously the conductivity of the rinse water itself has to be allowed for when taking readings. It is sufficient for tap water to be used for desalination, with deionised water being reserved for the final soak. Objects from marine sites may require a preliminary soak in diluted sea water in order to reduce the diffusion pressure. In the absence of a conductivity meter for monitoring the progress of salt removal, a sample of the wash water can be evaporated down until a small measured amount remains; assuming the salt has already been identified, the presence of the salt in the sample can then be checked using the appropriate salt test (see Appendix 2).

- *Soaking in running water*: for salt-contaminated objects in sound condition, flowing water can be used to dissolve and wash away the salts. Although quicker than using static water, this approach can demand large quantities of water.
- *Agitation soaking*: the wash water is gently agitated by an instrument thereby preventing the build-up of salts in the water immediately surrounding the object. This method takes a similar length of time to soaking in running water and uses less water.
- *Poulticing*: various poulticing methods such as paper pulp, Laponite RD, and Sepiolite, can effectively remove salts. The poultice is mixed with deionised or distilled water in the usual way, then applied to the surface of the pottery which may, or may not, have been pre-soaked (depending on the size and condition of the object). It is advisable to apply a separating layer of Japanese tissue to aid complete removal of the poultice material. As the poultice dries, the salts in solution are drawn into it and so removed. The process is much slower than any of the previous methods described and can be further prolonged by controlling the rate of evaporation through the use of polythene. The fact that much less water is used may be more desirable for low-fired wares or very large objects. Poultices should not be used on delicate or friable surfaces. Samples of the poultice can be soaked in deionised water and the salt content measured.
- *Ultrasonic cleaning*: the use of ultrasonic waves on submerged ceramics has been shown to be a more rapid method of salt extraction, but should not be used on friable ceramics or those that are cracked or structurally delicate.
- *Electrodialysis and electroendosmosis*: these are specialised techniques used to desalinate ceramic bodies with very small pore size. An electric current is passed between two stainless steel electrodes placed on either side of the submerged object. The salts migrate from the object into the water to form an electrolytic solution.

CHAPTER SEVEN

Consolidation

In certain situations where an object is extremely friable and at risk of breaking up, it may be necessary to introduce a consolidant to bind the constituents together. Common examples requiring such an approach include excavated objects from which the constituents have been leached away, or where the fabric has suffered disruption due to the absorption of soluble salts. Very occasionally, in special circumstances, an alternative option to consolidation – involving firing the ceramics to a low temperature – may be appropriate for unfired ceramics. However, the ethical dilemma of whether to follow such an approach, as for example in the case of cuneiform tablets, involving a radical alteration of the physical nature of the ceramic and the attendant risks associated with firing should be carefully balanced with the need to preserve important cultural information associated with the object.

The choice of consolidant

The main function of the consolidant is to hold the crumbling object together. This is achieved by either binding chemically to the particles of the substrate, or by forming mechanical reinforcement throughout the substrate without reacting with it. The primary ethical concern to both approaches is the reversibility of the resin and treatment, particularly where the application is to a fragile material which will inevitably suffer some degree of damage if removal of the consolidant is attempted. Also, when some types of resin age, cross-linking may occur which can cause shrinkage and discolouration. For these reasons, consolidation should be regarded as a last resort.

In selecting a consolidant the following points should be considered:

- *Penetration* is important if the consolidant is to reach the whole of the fragile structure. The extent of penetration will depend on a number of factors including: the size of the pores in the ceramic body, the size of the resin molecule, the solvent used, the concentration and the method of application. For objects in the field it may be preferable to apply some temporary consolidant to coat the surface of the object so that the object can be retreated later after the excavation.

  In situations where deep penetration of a friable unstable body is required, silane resins have been used. Desalination is possible following treatment. Silanes should always be used with caution as they are not reversible and are toxic if inhaled.
- *Appearance:* any change in the colour or texture of the surface of the object is undesirable and spot tests should always be performed first. Concentration of the resin, the solvent used and the rate of evaporation may affect the appearance.
- *Condition:* if the object is damp, a water-based resin system may be best, although if the object is very wet the consolidant may not dry sufficiently. In some instances it may be desirable to use a temporary consolidant such as cyclododecane, which sublimes at room temperature with continued air exposure, avoiding the need for later removal.
- *Environment* may play a part in the choice of a consolidant. The glass transition temperature of a resin is the temperature (Tg) at which it starts to change from a hard material to a soft one and will be critical in hot conditions where there is no environmental control available. If the glass transition temperature of the chosen resin is too low, the surface will become subject to dirt pick-up. Resins such as Paraloid B-72 (Acryloid B-72), which are so widely used in the UK and USA, would be less appropriate in the hot climates of India and South-east Asia unless environmental control was possible. Light stability of the resin should also be considered if high levels of UV radiation are envisaged.

Application of consolidants

Ideally the entire object should be consolidated simultaneously to avoid internal stresses. Consolidants are usually used at concentrations between 5% and 15% in order to ensure penetration. The volatility of the solvent will affect the degree of penetration, a more volatile solvent only allowing limited penetration. Penetration will also be improved by placing the object in the solvent vapour for 24 hours. The method of application and the way that the consolidant dries will also affect the absorption of the consolidant.

- A *brush* offers the simplest method of application allowing several applications of consolidant to be brushed onto the surface of the object until it no longer sinks in. On delicate surfaces, small amounts of the consolidant can be carefully dropped onto the surface, rather than brushing, which might disturb the surface.
- Using a *glass pipette* or *micro-pipette*, the consolidant can be precisely applied, drop by drop, onto the surface. This method is useful for localised consolidation where a greater degree of control is desirable.
- *Injection:* in certain instances it may be desirable to direct the consolidant deep into a crack or beneath an area of lifting glaze or body using a syringe.
- *Spray:* large areas can be quickly and evenly covered by spraying using a simple hand-held domestic mist spray. If a more controlled and focused application is necessary – for example, friable painted decoration – an airbrush can be used, although a compressed air supply will be necessary. Suitable precautions must be taken to protect the user from inhaling vapours.
- *Immersion:* the object can be placed on a metal or plastic rack and lowered into a container which is very slowly filled with consolidant. The object is fully submerged and the consolidant is gradually drawn into the body by capillary action. Penetration can be improved by exposing the object to an atmosphere of the solvent used in the consolidant prior to immersion. This method would not be appropriate for very fragile objects.
- *Vacuum impregnation* offers the most complete and thorough level of impregnation, but should only be reserved for those objects that can tolerate it. The object is placed in a vacuum tank on a metal or plastic rack and consolidant is applied very slowly as described above. The vacuum is then applied, sucking the air out of the pores and forcing consolidant in.

Drying

The method of drying plays an important part in achieving good results with consolidation. Rapid drying causes solvent-based systems to be pulled back out to the surface of the object as the solvent evaporates off. White blooms may occur as a result of water condensing on the resin as the solvent evaporates, cooling the whole system. Drying can be slowed down by placing the object in an atmosphere of the solvent for at least two days. Alternatively, the object can be placed in a polythene tent. Any residue can be removed with swabs of cotton wool and solvent. The consolidant must be completely dry before any further treatment otherwise it may interfere with the next stages.

CHAPTER EIGHT

Joining broken pieces

The earlier sections have shown that ceramic objects are susceptible to physical impact and are easily broken into pieces. In order to restore the aesthetic or functional value of the object and protect it from further loss or damage, it will be necessary to join the fragments back together in such a way that the joins are structurally stable and not overly visible. The process requires skill, experience and patience in order to achieve a good result.

Theoretical considerations

Prior to commencing the process of bonding, the conservator should assess the various factors that will determine the approach and choice of adhesive. The nature of the ceramic body will be one of the main considerations; a low-fired body is more porous in nature and likely to absorb more resin than a high-fired ceramic. On the other hand, the scale of the object may be such that it requires an extremely strong adhesive of a type that would normally not be appropriate for a low-fired ceramic. The choice of a suitable adhesive is dependent on the following parameters.

- *Strength:* the adhesive should be strong enough to hold the joined pieces together and tolerate handling. However, the adhesive bond should be slightly weaker than the ceramic body itself so that should the object be subjected to stress in the future, it will yield along the adhesive join rather than causing fresh damage.
- *Reversibility:* ideally the adhesive should be fully reversible without any risk of damage to the object. With low-fired porous wares it may be unrealistic to expect total removal of the adhesive. The more

soluble the adhesive, the more easily it can be removed. Adhesives such as epoxies and polyesters that cross-link on curing and are insoluble can only be softened and swelled by solvents. Their use would present a problem in a porous ceramic body, particularly where they have been absorbed into the body.

- *Viscosity:* the viscosity of an adhesive should be appropriate to the ceramic and the type of resin. An adhesive with very low viscosity applied to a non-porous surface will ensure a very tight join between two fragments; however, the same adhesive applied to a very porous ware would be sucked into the body, leaving very little adhesive behind on the surface resulting in a very weak bond. Absorption of the adhesive may cause shadowing behind the break and an undesirable strengthening effect on that part of the body: complete removal of the absorbed resin is likely to be difficult or impossible. The viscosity can be adjusted by altering the solvent-to-solid ratio, by adding fumed silica or, in the case of epoxy resins, allowing them to thicken slightly before application.
- *Appearance:* ideally the adhesive should be clear and colourless, although this may not be strictly necessary for all applications.
- *Shrinkage:* it should not shrink on curing or subsequently with the passage of time.
- *Long-term ageing:* the adhesive should be durable and stable in the environment to which it is likely to be exposed.
- *Application:* the adhesive should be easy to prepare and use. Some adhesives cure very rapidly and have a short pot-life (the amount of time the adhesive remains workable after mixing) which may be desirable in some circumstances, but a problem in others. If the adhesive has to be very precisely measured and mixed, errors are more likely to occur.
- *Availability:* it may be difficult or costly to obtain certain specialist adhesives locally and this may be a deciding factor for conservators working in remote areas.
- *Health and safety:* all the resins and solvents mentioned in this section are, to some extent, harmful to health. The user must pay close attention to the manufacturer's health and safety guidance, and take necessary protective measures. In the case of polyester and epoxy resins, particular care must be observed in their handling, avoiding skin contact and exposure to fumes as gradual sensitisation can occur with serious long-term effects.

Planning and preparation

Following on from thorough examination and cleaning of the damaged object, the process of bonding the pieces back together can begin. One of the most critical things to remember when commencing bonding is the importance of keeping everything clean; this applies to tools, worktop and hands. The merest particle of dust can spoil the overall result. It is important to prepare everything well in advance. The adhesive should be mixed and any support materials made ready. The whole process of bonding an object should be carried out in one sitting avoiding any interruptions. Completing the process in one session ensures that small readjustments can be made to the alignment if necessary.

Initially time should be spent establishing the sequence in which the pieces should be joined, paying particular attention to avoiding locking pieces out (Fig. 8.1).

A dry run of the assembly can be made with no adhesive, supporting the pieces with adhesive tape and numbering each fragment in order if necessary. The usual approach is to sort the fragments into groups, each group being assembled as a unit using at least one large piece as an anchor for the smaller fragments. The units are then joined together (Fig. 8.2). The approach to joining hollow vessel forms is more complex and requires

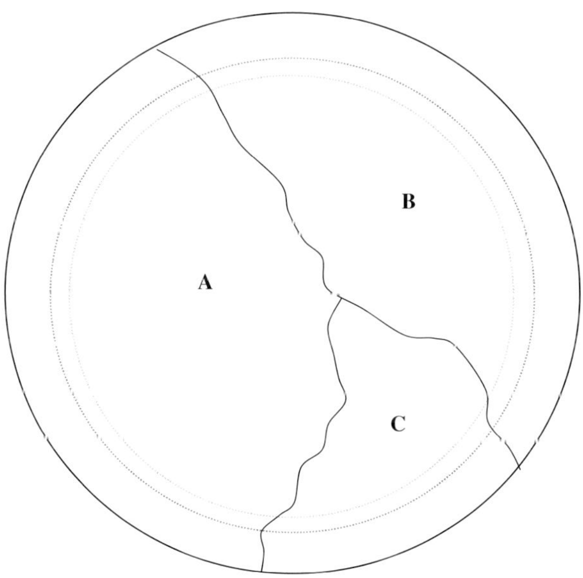

Figure 8.1 Order of joining pieces of a broken plate. If A and B are joined first, C will be locked out.

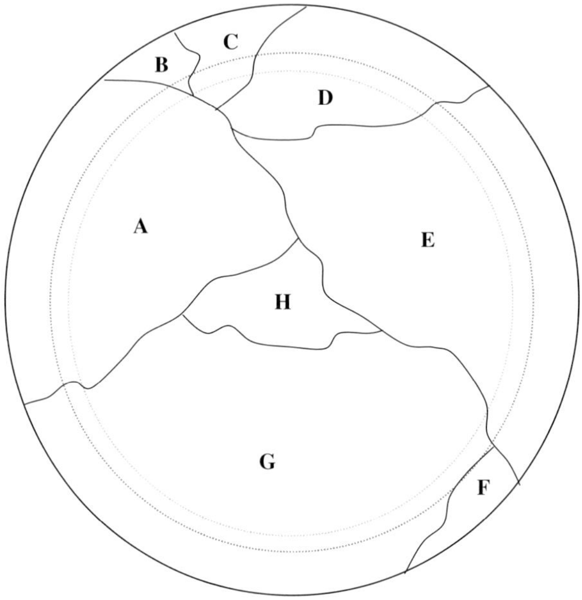

Figure 8.2 Order of joining for more complex damage. The fragments can be sorted into three groupls: A + B + C, D + E and F + G + H. Each group is assembled as a unit and then the three are joined together.

more thought than for flat ware. Previously restored objects should be drawn before dismantling, mapping the position of each piece.

It will usually be necessary to provide some form of support while the adhesive cures. This can be achieved through the use of short lengths of adhesive tape placed perpendicular to the break-edge, one on the front and a corresponding tape on the back. It is important to test that the pressure-sensitive adhesive on the tape is compatible with the bonding adhesive as some have adverse reactions that could cause undesirable colour changes in the resin. Matt or unglazed surfaces cannot be supported with tapes other than masking tape. Unless it is removed within a few days, masking tape will leave rubbery residues on the surface which can be absorbed by porous bodies. Elastic bands are sometimes used as an alternative means of support, although they are difficult to control. The whole object can be propped up on a tray filled with sterile sand, if necessary, isolated from the sand with thin polythene or tissue.

Choosing an adhesive

There are only a few adhesives available that fulfil the requirements outlined above, and of these only a small number have been specifically made for conservation. Those materials currently in use represent the best that are available. The nature of the ceramic body will largely determine the choice of the adhesive (Table 5.1). The following section covers the main groups of adhesives used for bonding ceramics and describes the method used in general terms.

The use of solvent-based adhesives

Many adhesives fit into this category including: the acrylic resins (e.g., Paraloid B-72 or Acryloid B-72, an ethyl methacrylate methyl acrylate copolymer) and the cellulose nitrates (e.g., HMG, Durofix and Duco Cement). These are usually used for bonding earthenwares, but may also be used for adhering porcelains and stonewares where a strong bond is not required. If the adhesives are likely to be exposed to high temperatures while on display it is vital to ensure that the glass transition temperature is well above the ambient temperature to avoid slippage. The resins are usually of a sticky nature which provides some degree of instant tack. Joins may be adjusted after the initial setting by re-wetting with solvent, or in some instances by applying gentle heat using a hot-air blower along the join.

There are various approaches to the application of the adhesive:

- The break-edges may be pre-wetted with the solvent prior to applying the adhesive to both halves of the break. In the case of porous bodies, it may be advisable to prime the break-edges before applying the adhesive using a (5–20%) solution of the adhesive, the concentration being dependent of the nature of the ceramic and the potential risk of staining. Priming in this way will help to seal the edges and encourage a stronger, more effective bond.
- The adhesive (40–50%) solution is carefully applied along the break-edge using a brush. In some instances application to one half may be sufficient, although application to both surfaces sometimes improves the tack.
- Initial adhesion is sometimes improved by bringing the two halves together, then pulling them apart briefly before finally reuniting them again and pressing them tightly together (an approach not appropriate for delicate or friable material).

- The assembled pieces can be supported with adhesive tapes as already described, which can be removed later after the solvent has fully evaporated.

The use of poly(vinyl acetate) emulsions

Poly(vinyl acetate) emulsion is a vinyl polymer that is used occasionally for bonding earthenware objects. However, its low glass transition temperature (room temperature) makes it susceptible to dirt pick-up and also to cold-flow where the joins lose their alignment. Consequently this adhesive would be inappropriate in hot climates unless environmental control could be assured.

1. The fragments are prepared as previously described and adhesive tapes applied as usual.
2. The break-edges must be dampened with deionised or distilled water in order to assure a strong join.
3. The milky emulsion is then applied to one of the break-edges and the two halves brought together, firmly squeezing out any excess emulsion.
4. The adhesive tapes are laid into position carefully. Accidental wetting of the tapes should be avoided as far as possible as this will prevent them sticking to the ceramic.
5. The nature of this adhesive makes it difficult to readjust the fragments after joining without the risk of weakening the bond.
6. After all the fragments have been joined the object should be set aside to dry for at least 48 hours until the water has had a chance to evaporate.
7. Excess adhesive can be cleaned away with damp swabs before curing, or with swabs of acetone or a scalpel after curing.

The use of epoxy resins as adhesives

Epoxy resins are usually reserved for low-porosity ceramics such as porcelain and stoneware. Extremely strong and hard, these adhesives are composed of a resin component which is mixed with a hardener. The curing time varies according to the type of epoxy system and the ambient temperature – some can take as long as seven days to reach full cure. Examples include Araldite AY103/HY956, Araldite 2020, HXTAL NYL-1, UHU-plus endfest 300 and Fynebond. Some require mixing in very precise proportions. The curing of some epoxy resins has been shown to be affected by cold temperatures and high humidity.

The epoxy hardeners tend to be toxic and potentially sensitising via the skin and respiratory system. Users with allergies, dermatitis or any sensitisation should avoid exposure to the uncured epoxy components by wearing protective gloves and mixing under extraction.

1. The prepared fragments are given a final swab with acetone to remove any remaining traces of dirt or grease from handling. The edges can be checked at this stage under a microscope to make sure that there are no hairs or fibres clinging to the edges.
2. The pre-cut prepared tape support strips should be applied to the smaller of the two pieces to be joined, at right angles to the break. The unattached end is pulled back out of the way. The strips are placed at intervals on the front and back of the break-edge directly opposing each other so that when the tapes are stretched across the join the induced stresses should be evenly balanced (Fig. 8.3).
3. The mixed adhesive is then applied to the larger half using a clean fine tool such as a cocktail stick or paint brush. Only a very small amount of adhesive need be applied – avoid the temptation to apply a

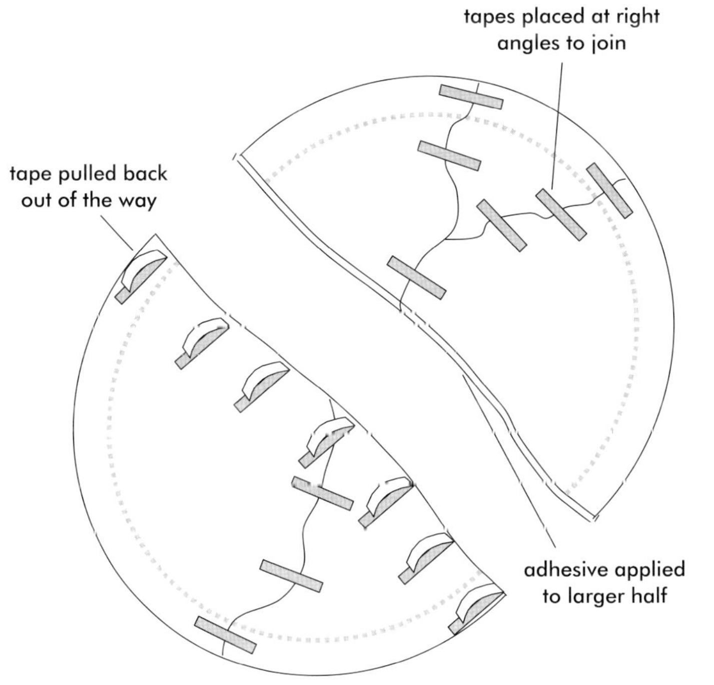

Figure 8.3 Bonding fragments together using adhesive tapes for support.

generous amount as excess adhesive will prevent tight contact and may lead to misalignment later.

4. The two fragments are carefully eased together. The alignment can be checked by running a clean fingernail over the join. Gentle pressure can be exerted to readjust the parts if necessary. When the two pieces are satisfactorily aligned, the pieces can be pressed firmly together and the strips of tape pulled across the join. Alignment can then be re-checked, the tapes lifted one at a time and tension applied evenly across the break thus pulling the two sides together. If the alignment is still not correct, the tape in that area can be re-stretched to redistribute the tension.
5. For repairs involving several fragments, the process can be repeated until all the fragments are reassembled following the previously determined order. It is important to keep checking the alignment to make sure that the joins are satisfactory. For hard-paste porcelains and delicate objects with multiple breaks, it may be preferable to assemble all the pieces with tape 'dry'. When assembly is complete a low-viscosity epoxy can be dotted into the joins. The resin will be drawn deep into the joins by capillary action. Any excess adhesive can be removed at this stage using a swab slightly dampened with IMS or acetone, but taking care not to flood the join as this will weaken the bond. Alternatively excess can be left to be removed later with a scalpel. When bonding porcelain, the epoxy can be tinted with titanium dioxide to reduce any shadowing effect along the joins.

Occasionally epoxy resins have been used on earthenware objects in situations when the size and weight of the object necessitated a very strong adhesive. However, they are not usually used on earthenware objects because complete removal without damage cannot be assured.

The use of polyester resins for bonding

Polyester resins are less commonly used on ceramics. They are available in two-part packs (consisting of a resin and an initiator) as low-viscosity liquids or thick thixotropic pastes. Polyesters tend to yellow on exposure to light and are vulnerable to moisture attack. The pastes are probably the most commonly used form of polyester for bonding ceramics (e.g., Sebralit and General) as they offer a rapidly curing mechanical join suitable for large objects with craggy edges. The parts can be supported by hand during the initial cure. This approach is usually unsuitable for multiple joins as all the stages have to be carried out quickly before the curing has become too far advanced. It is not possible to achieve such a thin application of adhesive on the break-edges compared with epoxy resins, although due to the nature of the large heavy coarse earthenwares on which they are generally used, this is not generally a problem.

For health and safety reasons, polyester resins must be handled under effective fume extraction to prevent exposure to the harmful fumes that are generated during curing. Gloves and eye protection should be worn to avoid contact with the uncured resin. The sterene component of the uncured resin is a highly toxic aromatic hydrocarbon solvent which can cause damage to internal organs. It is also a suspected carcinogen. Organic oxides may cause eye and respiratory irritations and many are sensitisers.

1. The adhesive is dotted along the middle of the break-edge.
2. The two parts are gently eased together until the correct alignment is found. Pressure is then applied to the two parts in order to squeeze out any excess adhesive and give a tight join.
3. The pressure must be evenly maintained on the join during curing (usually around 10 minutes for the initial cure).
4. Excess adhesive is removed while still soft with a scalpel, or with acetone while wet.

The use of cyanoacrylates

This group of acrylic adhesives includes the so-called superglues or instant adhesives. They are widely available and are marketed mainly for domestic applications. Their use in conservation has so far been limited due to concerns about their reversibility, however they have been used as a means of tacking stoneware or porcelain fragments together in situations where no other means of support is possible. The pieces must be positioned accurately as there is no scope for adjustment. It should be mentioned that the long-term ageing properties are poor and the stability of these adhesives has not been fully assessed.

The use of more than one adhesive

Occasionally there may be situations in which it is appropriate to use two different types of adhesive for the same job. An example of this is where an adhesive such as a cyanoacrylate is used to provide instant tack to support the join while an epoxy acts as the main adhesive strength. Dots of the cyanoacrylate are applied at intervals along the break-edge, and the two parts are joined and allowed to fully cure. A low-viscosity epoxy resin is then fed along the join and drawn into the crack by capillary action. Another example would be the use of a resin such as Paraloid B-72 in a 5–20% solution (depending on the absorbency of the body) to pre-prime the break-edges of an earthenware prior to applying an epoxy resin. The point of this approach is to reduce the risk of the epoxy being drawn into the porous body.

Consolidation of cracks

Cracks in ceramics are a common problem, which in some instances can present a real threat to the wellbeing of the object. If carelessly handled, a crack can easily travel to form a break. Securing the crack involves feeding a reversible adhesive along the line. The crack needs to be cleaned as thoroughly as possible by the various methods mentioned earlier. Solvent-based adhesives offer the most reversible option as a means of securing the two sides of the crack. The resin is painted along the crack repeatedly, and solvent can be washed over the resin to encourage it to flow deep into the crack. Glass capillary tubes may also be used to apply the resin. Other adhesives such as epoxies might provide stronger reinforcement, but would be virtually irreversible in the long term and their use should be avoided for crack consolidation.

Sprung and distorted cracks

Where tension exists in a ceramic body, a certain amount of distortion may occur when the object is damaged. A crack may release the tension allowing the object to relax into a slightly warped form. The edges of the crack will no longer line up and may be slightly stepped, requiring the application of pressure to force them back into position. However, by forcing the two halves of the crack back together, stresses may be set up elsewhere and it may actually be preferable to compromise and secure the crack by filling rather than applying pressure.

Dowelling

It may be necessary on occasions to use a dowel in order to provide extra structural support to hold the two parts in position. For example, when reattaching a broken limb onto a figure or re-joining a standing dish to its base. The process involves the rather contentious step of removing original material from the object by drilling holes into which the dowel is inserted. The ethics of undertaking such an approach should be very carefully considered before proceeding. A dowel may be the only option in situations where a join made with adhesive alone might fail and place the object at risk. This is generally appropriate where the break cannot provide enough surface area for the adhesive to support and connect the two parts safely. Where old dowel holes already exist, the holes can be reused.

The dowel itself should be made of a strong inert material such as stainless steel, Perspex (ICI) or Plexiglas, and its diameter should not exceed the thickness of the ceramic surrounding the hole. The two holes are drilled with a high-speed diamond-tipped drill. The hole should allow the dowel to fit snugly. After the first hole has been drilled the precise position of the corresponding second hole should be marked. It may be necessary to bend the dowel for a better fit; in the case of metal, this can be done with pliers while for Perspex and Plexiglas the application of heat will be required. Adhesive is then placed in each hole to secure the dowel and around the surrounding break-edge. Polyester and epoxy resins should be avoided in this situation due to the potential complications of reversing them should dismantling prove necessary at a later stage.

CHAPTER NINE

Filling missing areas

When a ceramic object is broken, some loss is almost inevitable. If this occurs along break-edges, the degree of loss may be very minor – particularly in the case of more durable wares such as porcelain and stoneware – but for friable and low-fired wares the loss may be more extensive. The gaps caused by missing material may leave joins exposed and vulnerable to further damage as well as the accumulation of dirt. Where large areas of loss have occurred, the reassembled object may still be structurally weak and visually incomplete. The usual approach is to fill such missing areas, although where there is no evidence on which to base a reconstruction – such as where a limb is missing, or a handle on a vessel – it may not be ethically acceptable to make up such areas. It may be more appropriate to leave them.

Other conservation disciplines such as textiles or furniture use matching fibres or wood to reconstruct areas of loss, however, in the case of ceramics, a similar approach, although technically possible, would be too complex and demanding to make it a realistic and economical option. Instead, synthetic fillers are used. These are made either from plaster-based materials or derived from resins such as epoxy, polyester and acrylic. In the same way that the choice of adhesive is determined by the type of body and the task in hand, a similar approach determines the use of a particular filling material. Those materials currently in use represent the best that are available. As with the adhesives, none have been specifically designed for conservation applications and they may have to be modified and adapted for use.

Filling materials

Generally, filling materials can be divided into two types: those used for filling low-fired porous wares and those for filling non-porous porcelain and stoneware.

Fillers for low-fired wares

Calcium-based materials have been used as fillers for low-fired wares for many years. Break-edges are usually sealed with a resin which is appropriate for the prevailing environmental conditions. A resin such as Paraloid B-72 can generally be used for this purpose. This should prevent the filler being absorbed into the body, not only weakening the join, but also making total removal difficult. The surface of the opaque white filling is usually retouched with a coloured medium to match the surrounding ceramic (Fig. 9.1). Ideally, it is better to avoid applying the filler directly to the object by making the filling away from the object, but this is only possible for larger areas of loss. The advantage of this approach is that the filling can be worked on, avoiding potential risk of damage to the object, and then attached later with adhesive. This can be achieved in various ways. One method involves isolating the area of loss using tin foil or a thin layer of plastic film to protect the object, enabling the filling to be made in the usual way and then removed for working. Alternatively, a model can be made in a suitable modelling material, such as wax, which can be carefully removed and cast in an appropriate material.

Plaster of Paris (calcium sulphate hemihydrate) has been used as a filling material for many years. There are several different grades of plaster available which may vary in their particle size, setting time, density, expansion and colour. Plaster is widely available, inexpensive, easy to use, fast setting, can be cut back, abraded and cast; it will also take paint well. However the main disadvantages are its short working and setting time, its difficult removal, and the possibility of causing salt contamination of the ceramic.

Polyfilla products are plaster-based proprietary fillers used by the building trade. They consist of modified mixtures of plaster of Paris. The interior grade version – most often used as a filler for earthenware – is made up of various ingredients including calcium sulphate, cellulose ethers and retarding agents. To use, it is mixed into a paste by adding water. It can

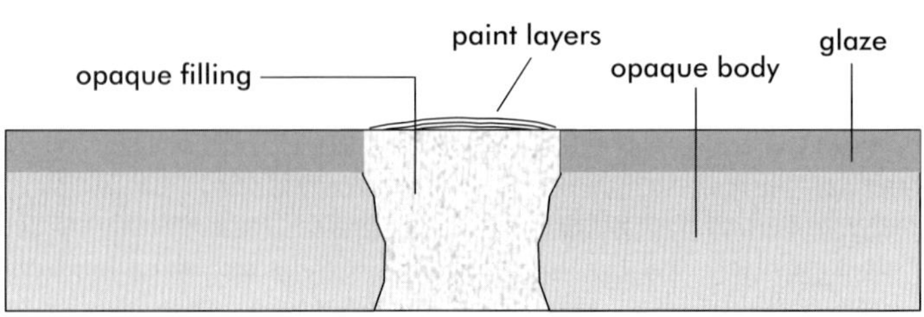

Figure 9.1 Section through an opaque plaster-based filling in an earthenware body covered with layers of retouching medium.

also be strengthened by adding a small amount of poly(vinyl acetate) emulsion. Fine Surface Polyfilla consists of a vinyl acetate reinforced plaster-based filler with added thickeners. Because of its very fine texture and shrinkage, it is used for surface finishing. Both plaster of Paris and All Purpose grade Polyfilla shrink to a small degree on setting, although this is fairly small. The density, strength and thermal expansion of plaster and Polyfilla match that of most earthenware bodies, making them good choices as filling materials.

The filler is applied using a small, clean, flexible metal spatula. Further filler can be added later to fill any small gaps or imperfections, and a final layer of Fine Surface Polyfilla may also be applied later. If a coloured filling is required, dry artists' pigments can be added to the dry plaster. Obtaining a precise colour match can be a laborious process, but it is worth taking time to make tests, mixing these with water then allowing them to dry thoroughly before comparing them against the object. The process can be speeded up by using a hot-air blower to dry the test samples. This approach can work well where the glaze is opaque or the body is opaque and unglazed (Fig. 9.2).

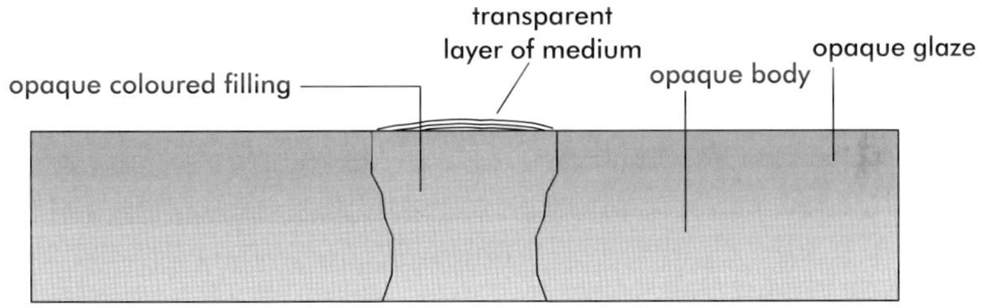

Figure 9.2 Section through body with opaque glaze the colour of the filling matched to the glaze.

A lightweight filling material made from acrylic resins (Paraloid/Acryloid B-72 and B-69) mixed with inert glass microspheres is sometimes used as an alternative to plaster-based materials. Recipes vary, but generally three parts of the microspheres are mixed with one part of the mixed resin. A 25–35% solution of the resin is usually made with appropriate solvents. For Paraloid/Acryloid B-72, a 50:50 mixture of acetone and alcohol (IMS or ethanol) is sometimes used. The alcohol slows down the speed of evaporation allowing more time to work the paste into the required form. The resulting filling is light, reversible, and easy to smooth using solvents.

Fillers for high-fired wares

The resins that are used to bond porcelain and stoneware, such as epoxy and polyester, tend also to be used as filling materials. They can be modified by the addition of various aggregates and pigments to alter their physical properties to suit the application. They can be bought commercially as ready-made filling materials or they can be mixed by the conservator. Various aggregates can be added to the resin; some (e.g., fumed colloidal silica, glass microspheres and marble powder) will produce translucent fills while others (e.g., French chalk (talc), barium sulphate and kaolin) give a denser more opaque effect depending on the amounts used. If the filling is carefully mixed so that it matches the colour and translucency of the original body and glaze, there will be no unsightly shadows and the filled area should not require any retouching. The putties and pastes made with resins produce very hard fillings when cured and it is often easier to do any shaping prior to curing. Once cured, the resins can be shaped by cutting, abrading, drilling or filing (Fig. 9.3). As previously mentioned, if the filling can be worked away from the object and reattached after the shaping and finishing has been completed, this will avoid any risk of damage to adjacent parts of the object.

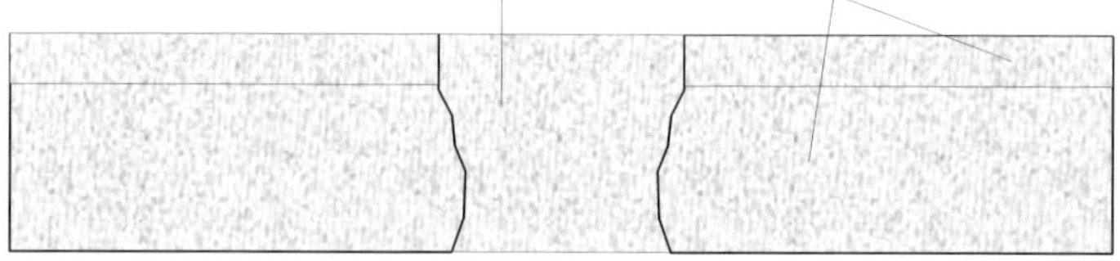

Figure 9.3 Section through a translucent porcelain body filled with a tinted epoxy filling.

Often the smaller losses that occur along the break-edges can be filled during the bonding stage, but for this to be successful the resin has to be tinted to match the ceramic surface. For larger chips, the prepared filling material is made by placing a small amount of resin on a clean white tile, and the aggregates then added. The choice depends on the desired effect, and the ratio of aggregate to resin will also vary accordingly. The filler should be easy to apply and stay in position. A test can be made by placing a small dot of the prepared filler in the area of loss to see how it looks. It may also be appropriate to build the filling up in layers, each layer imitating the qualities of the adjacent body and glaze (Fig 9.4).

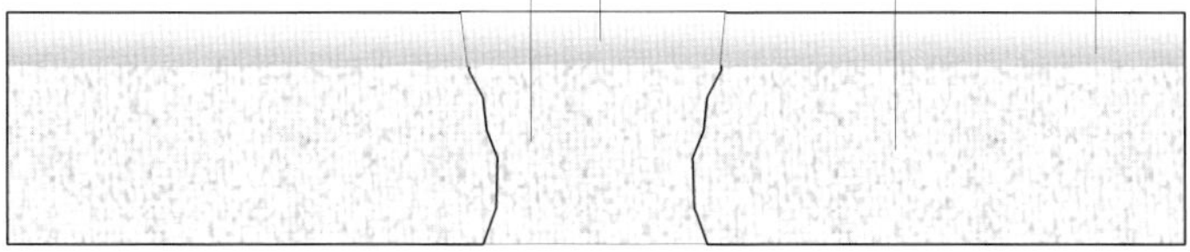

Figure 9.4 Section through a semi-opaque body with a transparent glaze. The filling has been applied in two layers to imitate the body and the glaze.

Filling chips and small losses

Small losses such as chips form the most common type of minor damage to ceramics, frequently at the rim of vessels or dishes. For larger chips it may be necessary to provide some support or backing for the filling material during curing. The simplest and crudest way of doing this is to use adhesive tape stretched over the filled area, squeezing the filler into shape. A variation on this when using thickened epoxy as a filler for porcelain and stoneware is to lay thin polythene or polyester film over the surface and gently coax it in place with a fingertip. When the film is removed a shiny surface is left which may not require any further work. However, for larger fills the results are rarely perfect, and such an approach is probably best reserved for minor chips.

A more accurate method of obtaining a curved filling is to take an impression of a corresponding intact area. A sheet of toughened dental wax can be softened with a hot-air blower or by immersion in hot water, and will faithfully reproduce curves although not the precise detail. The wax is placed on an intact area and pressed into position to take up the curve. It is allowed to cool, then carefully eased away from the surface. A gentle touch is required as the thin wax form can be easily damaged or distorted by careless handling. A separating coating of poly(vinyl alcohol) mixed with a drop of detergent can be applied to the surface of the wax and allowed to dry. It is then re-positioned over the damaged area (Fig. 9.5) and secured in place with adhesive tape (for porous surfaces), poly(vinyl alcohol) or by using a heated spatula to melt the wax and seal the edges onto the object (for non-porous surfaces).

The chosen filling material is then carefully applied. Dental wax should not be used in association with large amounts of epoxy or polyester resin due to the heat generated by these resins as they cure. When cured, the wax support can be removed. There may be some further work to be done in smoothing the filling down and filling small blemishes.

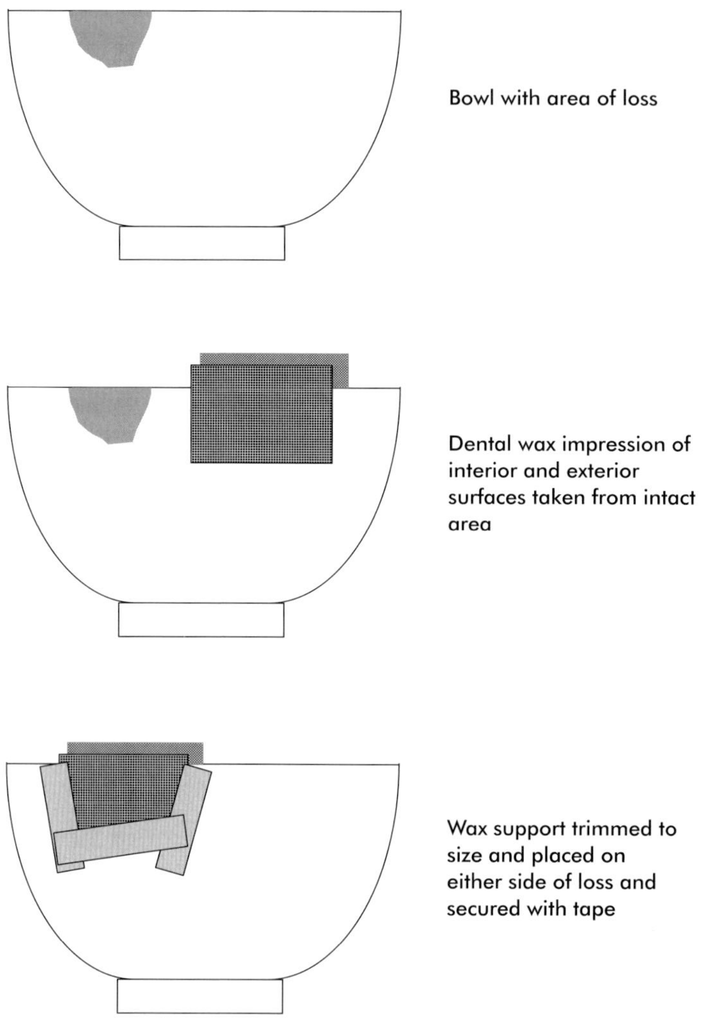

Figure 9.5 Dental wax being used to contain filling material while it hardens.

Larger gaps and holes may also be filled by adapting the above methods. Dental wax can be used on both sides of a hole to enclose the filling material and prevent it from leaking out. In such an instance each piece of dental wax will need to be thoroughly sealed onto the surface of the object in order to prevent the low-viscosity filling material from leaking. Two holes should be made in one of the wax walls: one to allow the filler to be injected into the cavity (using a syringe or a drinking straw) and the other to allow the air to escape.

Modelling

If there is no existing part from which to take a mould, the missing area can be modelled by hand provided there is sufficient evidence available such as photographs or similar objects. The modelling can either be done in one stage (directly on the object itself) or as a detachable fill in two stages. For fine delicate areas such as an arm or a finger, it may be easier to model directly onto the object over a wire armature. The armature can be inserted into an existing cavity or bonded directly onto the damaged surface. The option of drilling a new hole for the armature is generally regarded as ethically unsound as it would necessitate the removal of original material from the object and the inherent risks of damage. Ideally, in such instances the preferred approach is to build up the form using filler, allowing each layer to harden before the next application. For a detachable fill, the form is first modelled on the object with a soft material such as plasticine or modelling wax; the break-edge is protected during the process with a thin layer of plastic film. The resulting model is then removed from the object and used to make the mould from which a cast is taken to be attached to the object.

The use of moulds

Larger areas of loss may require a more complex method of filling by using moulds to make up the area. Moulds have the advantage of giving a result which is more faithful to the original. The process, however, depends on the existence of a part in good condition, identical to that which is missing, from which to take the mould. There are a number of approaches to moulding ranging from simple impression moulds to complex multiple part moulds. Flexible moulding materials are used to accommodate three-dimensional forms with small undercuts. Some of these materials are not suitable for porous wares due to the risk of staining.

Liquid rubber latex

Liquid latex is a cheap, versatile and highly flexible material which can be used to make simple two-part moulds. If necessary, it can be thickened with cotton flock, powdered paper or special latex thickener. The latex is dabbed onto the surface in a series of layers, allowing each application to dry for 20 minutes in between. The first 2–3 coats should be un-thickened latex. A large number of layers will make a thicker, less flexible mould. A mother-mould of plaster of Paris may be made if extra support is required. The rubber is then carefully peeled away from the surface or cut away with a sharp scalpel, then rejoined with latex. Talc may be used to avoid the risk of the mould sticking to itself. Moulds made of rubber latex have a limited lifespan and may start to break down quite rapidly.

Silicone rubber impression materials

Many silicone rubber impression materials have been developed for the dental profession and consist of a thick silicone rubber putty which is kneaded together with its catalyst into a ball and then gently pressed around the form (e.g., Reprosil, Steramould, and Copol-sil). They cure within minutes reproducing a flexible mould capable of a good detail. These materials make good one-part moulds. A cast can be made using an appropriate filling material applied directly to the object, or away from it, to be attached later (Fig. 9.6).

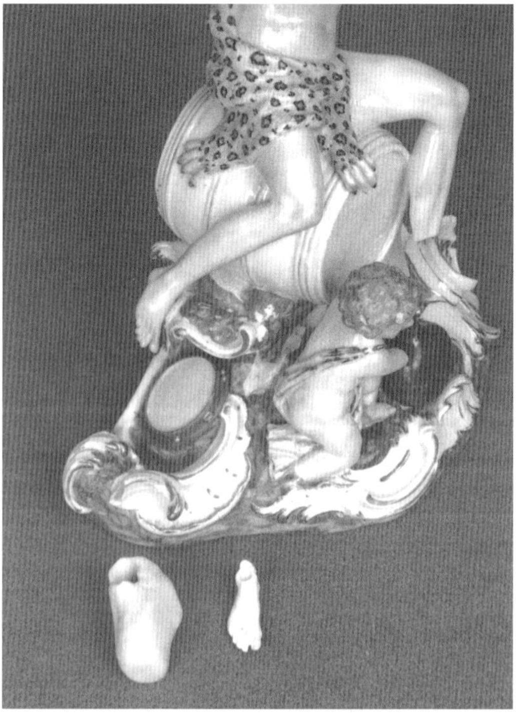

Figure 9.6 A one-piece mould of a foot on a figurine made with impression material.

Silicone rubber moulds

As well as impression materials, silicone rubbers are also available as moulding liquids which are ideal for making accurate piece moulds. Originally designed for industrial purposes requiring high-precision replication, they make excellent materials for ceramics conservation. These room temperature vulcanising (RTV) silicone rubbers cure by two different mechanisms: either by a condensation or addition reaction (e.g., Silastic 3110/916 which is condensation curing or Silastic E RTV which is addition curing).

(Precaution: before using any new or unfamiliar material, always carry out a small test on an inconspicuous part of the object. Silicone rubbers can mark or stain surfaces leaving a greasy residue behind. Certain condensation-curing silicones will adhere to glass and occasionally to glaze).

One-piece moulds

These can be made of small one-sided objects with minimal undercuts. The object is placed on a glazed tile or a sheet of glass. Any undercuts at the sides of the object can be filled with plasticine or modelling wax. A wall is then built up with wax or plasticine allowing a 1–2 cm margin around the item. An initial coating of the mixed silicone rubber is carefully painted onto the surface of the object; any air bubbles can be burst with a pin.

The initial layer can be left to semi-cure before pouring on the bulk of the silicone rubber to a thickness of 1–2 cm. Air bubbles can be encouraged to rise to the surface by gently tapping the table on which the mould is resting.

Two-piece moulds

These represent the next step in mould-making, where a complex three-dimensional form with undercuts requires a mould made of more than one piece. Common examples are moulds of handles or knops. The process involves a series of distinct stages (Fig. 9.7)

1. The part to be cast (e.g., a cup handle) is half embedded in a soft modelling material such as plasticine placed on a glazed tile. If one were to imagine the handle sliced exactly in half down its longitudinal axis, the cutting line would be the seam marking the limit of the plasticine.
2. A wall is built up around the item, leaving a 1–2 cm margin around it. Locating keys are pressed into the plasticine bed with the blunt end of a pencil.

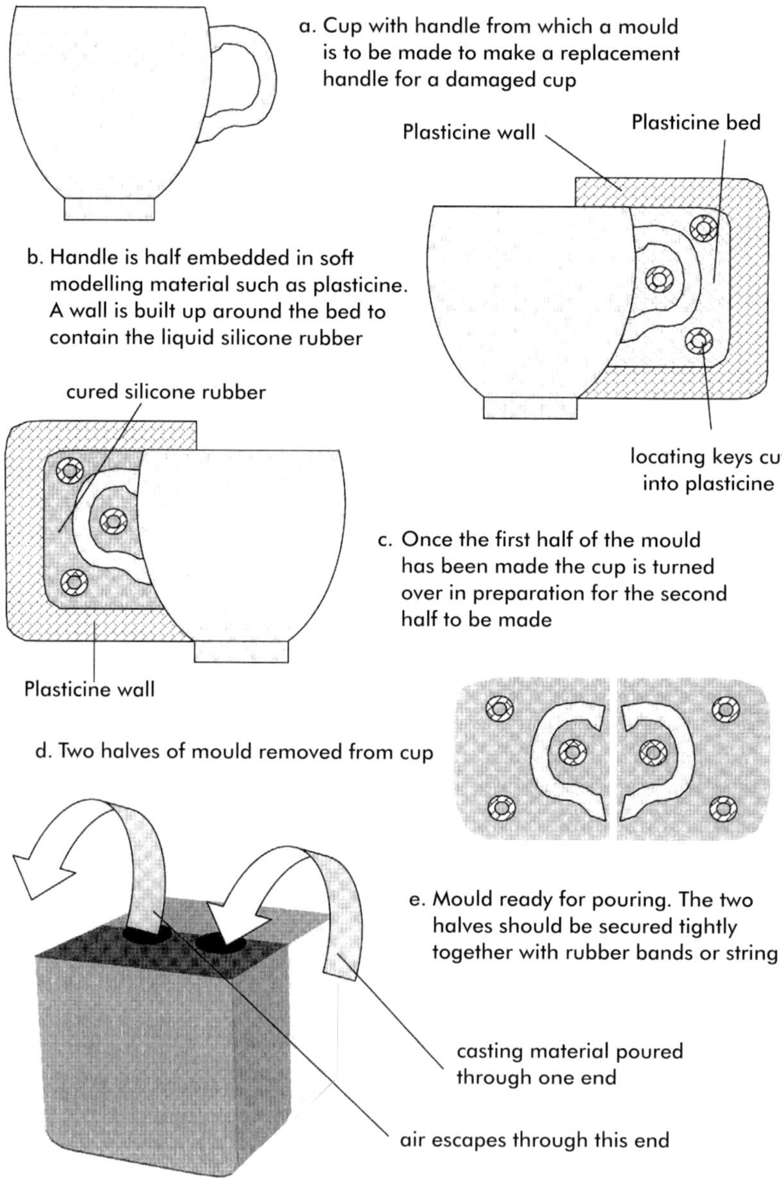

Figure 9.7 The stages in making a two-part mould of a cup handle.

3. An initial layer of silicone rubber is carefully painted over the surface of the object part, taking care to avoid air bubbles. This initial layer can be left to partially cure if time allows before applying more silicone rubber to a depth of 1–2 cm. The silicone is

left to fully cure.

4. The mould is then inverted, the tile removed, and the plasticine bed carefully eased away from the object. All traces of plasticine are cleaned off the silicone rubber and the object part, but leaving the wall in place. The enclosing wall is extended above the silicone taking great care to ensure there are no small gaps that might result in leaks.
5. A layer of release agent such as Vaseline is applied to the exposed surface of the silicone rubber mould.
6. The second side of the object part is now coated with silicone rubber as above and allowed to cure.
7. Finally, the plasticine wall is removed and the two halves are separated, releasing the object.

The next stage involves casting the form in resin or plaster. The two halves of the mould can be held together with rubber bands. In the case of a handle, the casting material is poured through the two handle stumps, or, for a knop, the stem is used as the pouring hole. Finally, the moulded parts are attached to the object with an appropriate adhesive and then finished to integrate them with the rest of the object.

There are numerous variations to the approach described above: plaster mother-moulds can be made to form an outer shell or a secondary mould to prevent distortion. If the entire item is being cast it will be necessary to include 'runners' made from plasticine to act as pour-holes for the resin. For particularly complex forms, multiple parts may be necessary and a certain level of skill and experience is required to master these.

Surface finishing

For all the filling techniques so far described, small flaws and irregularities are common: cutting back, rubbing down and polishing are therefore important stages in the finishing process. The junction between the ceramic and the filling is one area that nearly always requires further work. This stage is particularly important if the filling is to be painted as the retouching will highlight and draw attention to any blemishes. In the case of epoxy resin tinted fills, the surface will have to be carefully worked to a high standard by abrading and polishing. Ideally it is best to try to reduce the finishing stage as far as possible by careful preparation during the filling stage, and doing any necessary work on the filler before it hardens.

Materials such as epoxy and polyester once cured are very hard and resistant to cutting and abrading, whereas plaster and Polyfilla produce a relatively softer fill and are easily cut and abraded. There are many different ways to reduce and finish a filling, but it should always be remembered that used carelessly, all these methods can do irreversible damage to a ceramic by scratching or scraping the glaze surface. The most telling indication of lazy and unskilled work is damage by abrasion to the ceramic surface nearby.

- *Scalpels:* excess filling can be rapidly shaved or cut away with a sharp scalpel blade. Care must be taken not to be overly zealous and remove too much filling material – gradually remove one layer at a time. Scalpel handles number 3 and 4 with blades 23 and 15 respectively tend to be the most useful.
- *Files and riflers:* these will also remove large areas quite rapidly, however care should be taken to prevent the metal from coming into contact with the glazed surface. If necessary, the glaze can be protected with pieces of masking tape.
- *Abrasive papers and cloths:* various types and grades of sanding paper can be used to shape, level and smooth fillings, the most common being glass, silicon carbide and aluminium oxide. Very fine-graded cloth-backed abrasives such as Micromesh can be used for the final stages in smoothing and polishing. For use, the papers should be cut into small squares (1 cm). With careful precision, holding the square between the thumb and the forefinger so that only the corner makes contact with the surface of the filling, the abrasive is worked over the filling in short, controlled movements. Enormous care needs to be

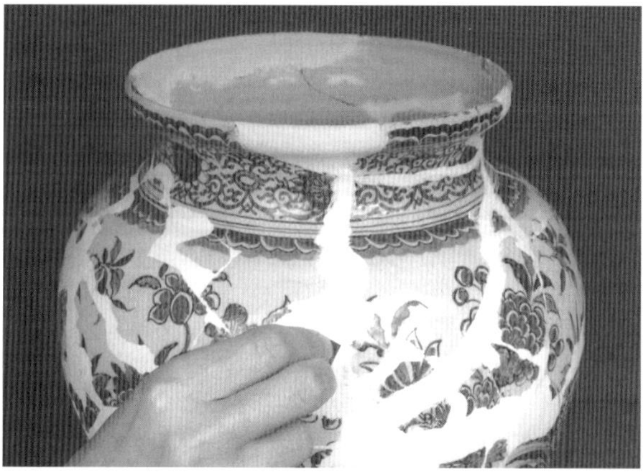

Figure 9.8 Rubbing down a fill with a small square of abrasive paper.

taken not to allow the abrasive paper to come into contact with the glazed surface, particularly in the case of silicon carbide and aluminium oxide, where the abrasive grits are actually harder than the glaze and are likely to cut into it (Fig. 9.8).

- *Polishing creams:* these consist of very mild abrasives such as kieselguhr suspended in a medium (e.g., Solvol Autochrome and Greygate Plastic Polish). They are applied using a bud of cotton wool and worked intensively in a circular motion; any residue is wiped away with an appropriate solvent.

CHAPTER TEN

Retouching fillings

Most of the processes described earlier prevent further damage to the object and as such constitute conservation. Filling missing areas and modelling described in the previous chapter can either be described as conservation or restoration depending on whether the new area fulfils a vital role in strengthening the object. However, the final retouching stage is not essential and therefore is really restoration. Retouching is used to hide fillings and restore the aesthetic integrity to the object. It should not be used as a way of concealing original material, for instance to hide chips or stains.

While some restorers working in private practice may aim for an 'invisible' finish, in museums or large private collections it is usually acceptable to aim for a finish that is unobtrusive and not distracting, yet still discernible to the trained eye. This is sometimes referred to as the 'six inch, six foot' rule, where a restoration which is visible at six inches disappears when viewed at a distance of six feet. The attainment of a totally invisible restoration can be very time-consuming and is ultimately misleading and dishonest. For collections with enormous backlogs of conservation to be done, it may be more sensible to agree to a policy on what is an acceptable standard.

Colour matching and lighting

The colour we see depends on the quality of the light that strikes the surface, the way the surface absorbs or reflects the incident light and the way the eye and brain interpret what it sees. Colour discrimination can vary widely between individuals. Most conservation training courses and employers now require candidates to pass strict colour vision tests as part of the selection procedure.

It is important to work in good lighting conditions. During winter months, the ideal lighting is natural daylight from a north-facing window. If possible, the object should be retouched in the same lighting conditions as those in which it is to be displayed to ensure a consistent colour match and avoid metameric effects (i.e. where colours appear to alter in different lighting conditions). Natural lighting can be supplemented by desk lamps and general overhead fluorescent lamps. Specialist tubes and lamps that simulate daylight conditions are available from good electrical suppliers

Retouching media

There are various media available for retouching ceramics, although none is truly ideal and each tends to lack one or more of the following essential qualities:

- complete reversibility and non-damaging to the ceramic substrate
- room temperature curing
- resistance to ageing
- good adherence to the filling
- hard finish that can be abraded and polished and is resistant to chipping during handling
- unchanged by additional applications of fresh media
- easy to apply with brush or airbrush
- safe to use and not hazardous to health
- appropriate colour
- good mixing and compatibility with dry pigments.

Acrylic paints and varnishes

Acrylic paints consist of pigment mixed with an acrylic binding medium. There are several different brands available (e.g., Cryla Colours by Rowney, Liquitex by Lefranc and Bourgeoise, and Winsor & Newton acrylic paints) made primarily for use by artists, and consequently they are widely available and relatively cheap and safe to use. To apply, they are mixed with water to the desired consistency and blended with other colours as necessary. They dry slightly darker than when first mixed, so it is necessary to allow for the colour change when mixing. Unfortunately the majority dry to a soft plastic finish, making them difficult to rub down except with the finest abrasives and polishes. They are well suited for use on a wide variety of ceramics, particularly archaeological and unglazed wares, although on fine porcelain the results may be disappointing.

Clear acrylic varnishes are available in gloss, matt or satin finishes (e.g., Golden varnishes). They can be pigmented with dry artists' pigments for use. They are water-based, safe and easy to use but have similar drawbacks to those described above.

Formaldehyde resins

Formaldehyde resins have been used in various forms as retouching media for many years (e.g., Rustins Plastic Coating and China Glaze). Their main advantage is that they produce a hard, brittle coating that can be abraded, polished and built up in layers to achieve effects closely imitating the ceramic glaze. Their main problem is their poor resistance to ageing and their harmful and hazardous nature, which requires them to be used under local exhaust ventilation.

Alkyd resins

Alkyds are used as an ingredient in some ready-mixed paints. They can be successfully used to retouch certain types of earthenware where a high-gloss finish is not required. For application they are diluted with white spirit. They set by evaporation of the solvent, producing a hard coating slightly darker in tone than when first mixed. They can be rubbed down with abrasive papers if necessary and are relatively resistant to light ageing, although they tend to yellow in the dark.

Bleached shellac

Bleached shellac is sold as 'white polish' and is often used as retouching medium for ancient Greek and Roman ware. Although slightly yellow in tone, water white clarity is not a problem on this type of ware. The resin is thinned as necessary with IMS and coloured with dry artists' pigments. It is generally worth persevering with the initial difficulties in mastering this particular medium as the results obtained on certain wares can be very sympathetic.

Epoxy resins

As well as the tinted fillings described earlier, epoxy resins can be applied as a final skin on both epoxy and plaster-based fillings to simulate a hard, glassy glaze. Dry artist's pigments and aggregates such as fumed silica can be added to modify the appearance of the resin and convincingly simulate glaze.

Colours

Some of the transparent media mentioned above can be coloured using various agents based on either pigments or dyes. Dyes tend to be less commonly used due to their intensity and potential to stain. Pure pigments, however, as dry finely ground powders, can be mixed with media to give almost any colour. Although the initial outlay can be quite high, pigments will last a long time provided they are lightfast and stored in sealed jars to prevent contamination. Artists' quality pigments tend to be more finely ground and lightfast. It is important that the pigments are compatible with the medium being used. Although there are lots of colours available, only a relatively small number are necessary to produce the colours of ceramic surfaces. An alternative approach is to use a pigment dispersion (e.g., oil paints) where the ground pigment is already mixed with a binder, although it is important to check the compatibility of the binder with the medium.

Matting agents

Although some retouching media are available in matt and satin finishes, most of the resins mentioned (with the exception of epoxy) can be modified by adding fumed silica to alter the reflectance qualities.

Abrasives and polishes

It is rarely possible to achieve a perfect finish when retouching: it will usually be necessary to smooth out the brush strokes or polish the surface. This can be done using the various abrasive papers, cloths and polishes mentioned earlier. In particular, the fine-grade polishing cloths such as

Ultrafine and Micromesh can be extremely useful at this stage. Polishing creams, such as Solvol Autochrome or Greygate Plastic Polish, will bring up a higher brilliance and microcrystalline wax will improve the gloss and fill in minor scratches.

Brushes

There are two options open to the conservator for applying paint to fillings: the artists' paintbrush or the airbrush. Both approaches require skill and experience in handling. The airbrush, which will not be covered in any detail here, is useful for covering large areas quickly and also for coating restorations that have been made away from the object as a detachable fill. Using the airbrush, the edge of the retouched area can be softly merged into the surrounding ceramic surface. The temptation, however, with such an approach is to spread the retouching out over a wider area thus covering the original surface and misleading the viewer. The artists' paintbrush, on the other hand, is easier to control. Apart from the initial expense of the airbrush itself, there is also the additional consideration of the compressed air supply and a spray booth for solvent extraction. By comparison, paintbrushes are cheap, widely available and easy to maintain; an airbrush will require meticulous cleaning and regular servicing if it is to be reliable.

It is worth investing in good quality artists' paintbrushes rather than cheap inferior quality imitations. They will perform better, last longer and give a better finish. Best quality sable or a sable-synthetic mixture should be used for all retouching. If properly cared for they will last a long time without shedding bristles. The aggressive nature of some retouching media and solvents may affect some synthetic brushes. Brushes with shorter bristles, such as those used by painters of miniatures, tend to be more suited to retouching media. A range of different sized brushes will give a choice for different jobs, but the most useful are likely to be no.1 and no. 0. Larger brushes will obviously be more useful for achieving coverage and finer ones for small detail. However smaller brushes will dry more quickly and will not hold as much media.

After use, the brush should be thoroughly cleaned in solvent to remove all the paint particles, then rinsed in warm soapy water. After blotting dry on tissue paper the tip should be gently eased to a point.

The method of retouching

Before starting retouching, it is worth deciding exactly what sort of result is required. If the fillings are not to be totally disguised but just made less obvious, they can be retouched to a colour that approximates with the general background. The colour should be kept slightly lighter. However, if a less visible result is required it will be necessary to start by painting a background colour that must be very closely matched to the ground colour of the ceramic. Decorative effects such as transparent or tinted glaze, enamel or gilding can be added only when the initial base colour is perfect. Although in theory the process sounds fairly easy, in practice it can be infuriatingly difficult (Fig. 10.1).

1. *Preparation:* all surface tools, equipment and hands should be spotlessly clean before commencing retouching. The medium should be mixed (if necessary) in a clean, lidded vial.
2. *Sealing the filling:* porous fillings made from plaster-based materials should first be sealed with a resin such as Paraloid B-72 (Acryloid B-72) or shellac. The coating will consolidate and strengthen the filling.
3. *Base layers:* for light-coloured bodies the first layers of retouching media should be mixed with generous amounts of white pigment. The pigment serves to thicken the coating, fill any small pits or scratches and helps even out the base colour. This first layer will also highlight any inadequacies in the surface of the fill. After hardening, any irregularities can then be gently rubbed down with abrasive papers revealing high spots and disclosing low areas. Flaws can be filled with

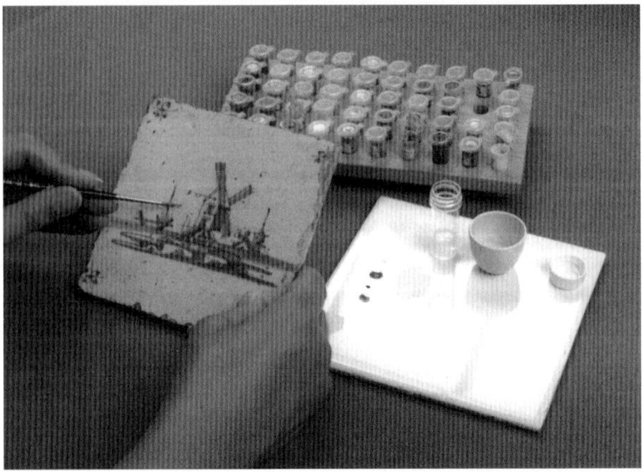

Figure 10.1 Retouching a filled area on a Delft tile.

blobs of retouching medium mixed with talc or with a fine filling material such as Fine Surface Polyfilla. Further layers can be applied until a perfect result is achieved.

4. *Background colours:* the most time-consuming and exacting part of retouching is achieving the background colour and making it fade imperceptibly into the surrounding surface. The colours and the medium are mixed together on a white glazed ceramic tile. Some coarser pigments may need grinding down in a little medium with the tip of a palette knife. Colours can be mixed with a palette knife or old paintbrush. The process of mixing colours can be very wearing on brushes and it's a good idea to save old ones for this job; however, they must be clean and free of loose hairs. The paint should be mixed quickly, keeping it gathered in a pool and not allowing it to dry. It is advisable to mix more than might be needed in order to allow for the wastage during the mixing process. Tests can be made on a spare scrap of filling material (saved from earlier), comparing it to the ceramic.

   When applying paint, the usual procedure is to fill in the edges first, working inwards towards the middle. On glazed ware, the extreme edge of the paint can be feathered out using a brush dipped in clear un-pigmented resin or solvent, taking care not to extend the paint any further than is necessary. The temptation to rework the surface of the freshly applied paint should be avoided as it will ruin the even finish.

   With time and practice, individual conservators develop their own ways of doing things. However, the basic tenets remain the same: aiming for an even background colour by building up a series of layers, rubbing down between each application with progressively finer grades of abrasive paper and cloths. After rubbing down, the background colour will appear lighter, but it will darken again with further polishing or after a gloss coating is applied.

5. *Decoration:* where there is sufficient evidence it will usually be acceptable to paint in any decorative features. In some instances, if the area is too extensive and the existing decoration too random, it may only be feasible to fill a small amount such as banding lines or repeating motifs. Chapter 1 briefly explained the different approaches to decorating ceramics. When trying to reproduce these it will be necessary to imitate the sequence to some extent. For example, for underglaze colours, the colours should be applied under the layers of transparent or tinted medium. Overglaze enamels can be painted on in the final stage and are often easier to copy because many were originally hand-painted by brush before firing. Because of the vast range of decorative finishes that exist on ceramics, their successful imitation depends largely on the ingenuity of the restorer. For complex patterns it may be

necessary to take a tracing of the pattern from elsewhere, then carefully transfer it to the paint surface.

Gilding and metallic finishes

Gilding was usually the very last process to be performed. Generally speaking, early unfired gilding on historic objects made prior to the middle of the eighteenth century rarely survives. However, examples of ancient Greek and Egyptian gilded objects exist which have remained remarkably stable. Later gilding, though fired, is still vulnerable to wear. Similarly lustre is another type of on-glaze decoration consisting of an extremely thin film of metal fired onto the glaze. There are many ways of simulating metallic finishes, although because of the reflective properties it is technically difficult to achieve convincing results.

For gilded areas, without doubt the best materials to use are gold leaf and powder gold. There are other alternatives available including acrylic gold paint, gold enamel colours, gold ink, gold pens, bronze powder, bronze paint and tablet gold, but they tend to give poor finishes, and where bronze powders have been used, they discolour and tarnish with time unless sealed. Although extremely expensive, gold leaf can give very realistic results. Fillings have to be absolutely perfect as the gold leaf tends to emphasise every small imperfection. The leaf can be adhered to the surface using one of the following approaches:

- Oil size is used by furniture and metals conservators to adhere gold leaf. The size is painted onto the surface and allowed to slowly dry and flatten to a perfectly smooth but tacky surface. The leaf is then carefully transferred with a brush or gilder's tip.
- Alternatively, gelatine dissolved in water can also be used to attach gold leaf, giving a very good result. Once the water has dried, the remaining gelatine forms a very thin layer between the fill and the gold. It is quicker to apply and easier to use than oil size and may be burnished with polished agate if required.
- Finally, retouching medium will also provide a base, although it tends to be less satisfactory because of the risk of brush strokes and the danger of damaging the surface below if a mistake is made and the gold has to be removed.

Transfer gold, which consists of gold leaf attached to a tissue backing, can also be attached to the surface with oil size. Transfer gold has the advantage of being easier to handle, and can be pre-cut with scissors to the desired shape.

Tablet gold consists of finely ground gold mixed with gum and is applied like water colour. It can be used for fine lines and dots but not large areas. It tends to produce a rather granular speckled finish.

Powder gold is very finely ground gold and is available in various shades depending on the proportion of gold to copper and silver in the mix. Good results can be achieved by lightly dusting the powder onto tacky oil size or retouching medium.

Silvering may be reproduced using silver or platinum leaf. The leaf has to be sealed with a cellulose nitrate lacquer to prevent tarnishing.

For lustreware, commercially produced lustre pigments composed of mica particles combined with pigments can give reasonable effects when mixed with retouching media. The use of bronze, gold or aluminium powders for lustre finishes can also be quite effective. Bronze powders can be mixed with retouching media for lustreware; the ratio of powder to medium should be high, although the finish tends to be rather grainy. The attainment of good results, not surprisingly, depends on experimentation and testing.

Occasionally a grey metallic sheen may be required to simulate the blackened burnished surfaces found on some low-fired wares. This can sometimes be achieved effectively by using fine particles of carbon as graphite powder from pencil lead.

APPENDIX 1

Treatment implications of different types of ceramic

	Earthenware	Stoneware	Porcelain
Average firing temperatures (°C)			
Biscuit	850–1150	950–1000	900–1000
Glaze	750–1100	1200–1300	900–1400
Characteristics	Porous, weak body. Clay particles only slightly fused. Glaze adds strength and a waterproof layer. Usually thick-walled and brightly coloured.	Hard, strong body with minimal porosity. Colours more subdued.	Virtually non-porous with white, often semi-translucent, body.
Typical deterioration problems	Staining, salts, mechanical damage (breaks, cracks, loss and chips), glaze loss.	Mechanical damage (breaks, cracks, loss).	Mechanical damage (breaks, cracks, loss).
Cleaning	Care required due to risk of staining and further damage where glaze is unstable, flawed or absent. Minimal wetting, use swabs and solvents where necessary. Poultices may be required for removing deep stains. Dry-cleaning techniques for unglazed wares.	Aqueous treatments may be used, also other solvents where necessary. Steam cleaning may remove ingrained dirt.	Aqueous treatments and other solvents may be used. Steam cleaning may lift ingrained dirt. Hydrogen peroxide will bleach organic dirt. Enzyme treatments may assist in removal of organic residues.
Removal of old fills	Preferable to use mechanical methods where possible avoiding unnecessary wetting of the body (and risk of staining).	Solvents may be used to soften or dissolve filling materials, then removed with mechanical methods or with a steam cleaner. Beware of resins such as shellac which may leave stubborn residues and stains.	As for stoneware.
Consolidation	Problems range from cracks to friable bodies and flaking decoration. Use easily reversible solvent-based resins applied locally by brush, pipette, or immersion and vacuum impregnation (severe cases).	Problems may include cracks or flaking decoration. Always use an easily reversible solvent-based adhesive applied locally with brush or pipette.	See stoneware.

(continued overleaf)

	Earthenware	Stoneware	Porcelain
Bonding	Easily reversible solvent-based adhesive.	Solvent-based adhesives, epoxy and polyester resins.	Epoxy resins
Filling	Plaster-based materials. Solvent-based resins bulked into a paste with aggregates.	Coloured fillings in epoxy resin with appropriate aggregates. Coloured plaster-based fillings.	Coloured epoxy resin mixed with appropriate aggregates. Occasionally coloured epoxy applied over plaster-based fillers.
Retouching	Acrylic paints, urea formaldehyde resin, bleached shellac, alkyd paints.	Acrylic paints, urea formaldehyde resin, coloured epoxy resin.	Coloured epoxy, acrylic paints, urea formaldehyde resin.

APPENDIX 2

Tests for salts

The wash water obtained when desalinating objects containing salts can be tested to detect the presence of sulphates, chlorides and nitrates. Alternatively it may be possible to remove a sample from the object prior to desalination and dissolve it in distilled water.

Chlorides

1. Dissolve sample in distilled water.
2. Place 10 ml of the made-up solution in a test tube.
3. Add 3 drops of dilute nitric acid to remove carbonate ions.
4. Add 3 drops of molar silver nitrate solution.
5. A white precipitate indicates chlorides are present.

Nitrates

1. Dissolve sample in distilled water.
2. Acidify solution with dilute sulphuric acid.
3. Place 10 ml in a test tube.
4. Add and dissolve a few fresh crystals of ferrous sulphate.
5. Slowly trickle a few millilitres of concentrated sulphuric acid down the side of the tilted test tube.
6. A brown ring indicates that nitrates are present.

Sulphates

1. Dissolve sample in distilled water.
2. Place 10 ml in a test tube.
3. Add a few drops of hydrochloric acid.
4. Add a few drops of barium chloride solution.
5. A white precipitate will be observed if sulphates are present.

Insoluble salts

Deposits of insoluble salts are usually carbonates, sulphates or silicates, either combined or on their own. When a small drop of dilute acid is placed on the deposit, a violent reaction will suggest carbonates while less vigorous effervescing would indicate sulphates. Silicates are not affected by most acids.

APPENDIX 3

Further reading

Acton, L. and McCauley, P. (1996) *Repairing Pottery and Porcelain*. London: Herbert Press.

Buys, S. and Oakley, V. (1996) *The Conservation and Restoration of Ceramics*. Oxford: Butterworth-Heinemann.

Charleston, R. (1981) *World Ceramics: An Illustrated History from the Earliest Times*. London: Hamlyn

Clydesdale, A. (1990) *Chemicals in Conservation: A Guide to Possible Hazards and Safe Use*. Edinburgh: Scottish Society for Conservation and Restoration.

Cronyn, J. (1990) *The Elements of Archaeological Conservation*. London: Routledge.

Dorrell, P. G. (1989) *Photography in Archaeology and Conservation*. Cambridge: Cambridge University Press.

Dowman, E. A. (1970) *Conservation in Field Archaeology*. London: Methuen.

Evetts, E. (1983) *China Mending: A Guide to Repairing and Restoration*. London: Faber.

Halahan, F. and Plowden, A. (1987) *Looking After Antiques*. London: Pan Books.

Hamer, F. and Hamer, J. (1986) *The Potter's Dictionary of Materials and Techniques*, 2nd edn. London: A and C Black.

Hodges, H. (1964) *Artifacts: An Introduction to Early Materials and Technology*. London: John Baker.

Horie C. V. (1987) *Materials for Conservation*. London: Butterworths.

Kingery, W. D. and Vandiver, P. B. (1986) *Ceramic Masterpieces: Art Structure and Technology*. New York: Free Press.

Kingery, W. D., Bowen, M. K. and Uhlman, D. R. (1975) *Introduction to Ceramics*. New York: Wiley.

Larney, J. (1975) *Restoring Ceramics*. London: Barrie and Jenkins.

Pearson, C. (1987) *Conservation of Marine Archaeological Objects*. London: Butterworths.

Rado, P. (1988) *An Introduction to the Technology of Pottery*. Oxford: Pergamon Press.

Rhodes, D. (1977) *Clay and Glazes for the Potter*, 2nd edn. London: Pitman.

Sandwith, H. and Stainton, S. (1993) *The National Trust Manual of Housekeeping*. Harmondsworth: Penguin Books in association with The National Trust.

Savage, G. and Newman, H. (1976) *An Illustrated Dictionary of Ceramics*. London: Thames and Hudson.

Sease, C. (1987) *A Conservation Manual for the Field Archaeologist*. Los Angeles: University of California.

Shelley, M. (1987) *The Care and Handling of Objects: Practices in the Metropolitan Museum of Art*. New York: Metropolitan Museum.

Stowlow, N. (1986) *Conservation and Exhibitions: Packing, Transport, Storage, and Environmental Considerations*. London: Butterworths.

Thomson, G. (1986) *The Museum Environment*, 2nd edn. London: Butterworths.
Watkinson, D. (ed.) (1987) *First Aid for Finds*, 2nd edn. London: RESCUE and UKIC Archaeology Section.
Williams, N. (2002) *Porcelain Repair and Restoration*. London: British Museum Publications.

APPENDIX 4

Glossary of ceramic terms

ball clay – clays possessing high plasticity due to their very fine particles. Light in colour. Added to other clays to improve plasticity.

biscuit firing – the initial temperature firing that usually precedes the glaze firing.

biscuit ware – unglazed ware that has had one firing.

body – the fundamental clay-derived component of a ceramic object as distinct from the glaze, slip or other decorative layers.

bone china – an English type of porcelain which contains 50% bone ash as a flux.

ceramic – general term for all products made of fired clay.

china – an imprecise term sometimes used to cover all types of porcelain and white earthenware.

china clay – the purest type of naturally occurring clay. It is an essential constituent of porcelain and bone china. Its composition is very close to the mineral kaolinite.

clay – hydrated silicate of alumina which occurs naturally as a plastic material that will retain its shape when dried and is altered by heat into a hard, brittle material.

coiling – a simple method of building a vessel using long coils of clay.

combed decoration – a pattern created by dragging a comb-like tool through alternating colours of wet slip. The result is a series of parallel wavy lines.

cover – another term for a lid.

crackle – a fine network of cracks within the glaze which are an intentional part of the decoration, most commonly occurring on Japanese and Korean ceramics. They are often deliberately stained by the artist to emphasise their visual effect.

crawling – a type of glaze defect where the glaze shrinks back leaving a bare patch of unglazed body.

crazing – a glaze defect consisting of a network of fine cracks caused by the tensions arising when a glaze contracts more than the underlying body.

dunting – cracks arising from stresses induced during firing and subsequent cooling.

earthenware – low-fired ceramics with a porous body. Objects tend to have thicker walls than porcelain and stoneware in order to compensate for their fragility. Exposed or broken edges tend to be rough with pores, ranging in colour from creamy-white to red-brown and black. When glazed, the otherwise porous ware is made waterproof. The glaze forms a distinct layer covering the underlying body and is often weakly attached. The decoration can be bright and colourful.

enamel – sometimes also referred to as on-glaze or overglaze enamel. It consists of mixtures of metallic oxides ground with frits containing a high proportion of fluxes such as lead, sodium and potassium. Application is onto the already fired glaze which is then heated to a relatively low temperature. Enamels tend to be softer than the glaze and consequently more prone to wear.

feldspar – a group of minerals containing alkali, silica and alumina which act as fluxes in both bodies and glazes.

firing – the process involving heating clay in a kiln or fire to convert it to ceramic.

flux – an oxide added to clays and glazes which has the effect of lowering their melting point.

frit – a material which is added to glazes, enamels and bodies to encourage vitrification. It consists of a glassy material that has been fired, cooled then ground down to a powder.

gilding – gold decoration applied to ceramics by various methods. Early historic gilding prior to the mid-eighteenth century was unfired and consequently very vulnerable to wear and moisture. Honey gilding involved mixing ground gold with honey prior to application to the ware, which would then be fired to a low temperature. Mercuric gilding is where gold is amalgamated with mercury and applied by brush. Modern methods of gilding are more durable.

glaze – a coating of glass which has been melted onto the surface of a ceramic body. It acts as an impervious hygienic layer giving strength to the object while also serving as decoration.

grog – powdered fired clay which is added to bodies to give texture, improve resistance to thermal shock and reduce shrinkage during firing.

hard-paste porcelain – sometimes referred to as true porcelain. Consists of a dense, white, non-porous, glassy body. The classic composition consists of 50% china clay, 25% feldspar and 25% quartz or flint.

in-glaze colours – decorative colours that are applied to the unfired glaze which then merge into the glaze during firing.

jiggering – a method of forming flatware such as plates. A metal profile cuts and shapes the clay on a revolving plaster mould.

jollying – a technique for forming vessels using a revolving mould to shape the exterior surface while a metal profile forms the interior.

kaolinite – the idealised clay mineral. A white crystalline mineral which is an important constituent of china clay.

kiln – the oven in which clay, glazes and decoration are fired to render them permanent.

knop – the finial, knob or handle on a lid.

leather-hard – describes clay which has been dried to a stage when it resembles leather, being stiff but flexible, and damp enough to be joined to other pieces with slip.

lustre – a metallic decorative effect consisting of an extremely thin deposit of metal. Lustre decoration tends to be vulnerable to wear and abrasion.

marbled ware – a decorative effect where two different coloured clays are partially mixed giving swirling patterns within the body.

on-glaze colour (overglaze colour) – another name for enamel decoration.

pinching – a simple technique for forming a pot by squeezing the clay into the desired shape, building up the walls by pinching the clay between the thumb and forefinger.

porcelain – a generic term for non-porous ceramics which have a white body. Objects are often semi-translucent. They can be decorated with colours under the glaze and with enamels on top of the glaze. Small objects tend to have thin walls. When struck they give a clear ringing tone. Exposed or broken edges can be very smooth and almost glassy in texture.

porosity – the property which allows a fired body to absorb liquids by capillary action. A low-fired earthenware is much more porous than porcelain due to the network of small pores within the body. In porcelain the spaces are filled with glassy materials.

pottery – objects made from fired clay. The term includes earthenware, stoneware and porcelain.

primary clay – also known as residual clay. The term applies to clay deposits which are found in the place of origin.

quartz – the common name for silica, one of the most commonly occurring minerals in the earth's crust. It has a very high melting point of 1710°C and is a vital constituent of all clays and glazes. Examples include sand, flint and rock crystal.

salt-glaze – a glaze formed from common salt. The salt is thrown into the hot kiln where it vaporises, the sodium combining with the alumina and silica in the clay to form a glaze.

secondary clay – also known as sedimentary clay. The term describes a clay which has been transported from its place of origin and deposited elsewhere. It is less pure than primary clay.

silica – silicon dioxide, a mineral which is the most important constituent of glazes. It is also an integral component of clay. It has a melting point of 1710°C.

slabbing – a method of constructing a pot using sheets of leather-hard clay joined together by scoring and applying slip.

slip – a liquid suspension of clay mixed with other ingredients in water.

slip-casting – a method of forming objects using slip and plaster moulds. The mould is made from an original model and the technique allows the possibility of mass production.

soft-paste porcelain – a high-fired ceramic with a dense, white, brittle body. The firing temperature is lower than that of hard-paste porcelain and the body is more porous. Exposed broken edges tend to be sugary in texture.

sprigging – the application of decorative elements or additional parts onto the main part of the object. The point of attachment on the object is scored, coated with slip, then the parts are applied.

stoneware – ceramics which are hard, durable and vitrified with a non-porous body. Objects can be glazed or unglazed and tend to be less thickly potted than earthenware objects. The maximum firing temperature is 1300°C with the body and glaze maturing at the same time producing a well-developed glaze-body layer. The glaze colours tend to be muted and less colourful than earthenware. Exposed or broken edges are compact and smooth.

terracotta – a type of ceramic made of a red-coloured clay.

throwing – the process of making pottery on a spinning wheel. A lump of plastic clay is centred on the wheel, then gradually, the potter makes an indentation in the lump, all the time keeping the clay lubricated with water. The form is gradually opened up and the sides of the vessel lifted up from the clay.

tin-glaze – traditionally a lead glaze which is opacified with tin-oxide and fired to earthenware temperatures. Wares are also known as maiolica, faience and delftware.

transfer print – a method of transferring a printed decoration from paper onto the ceramic. The pattern is printed using a mixture of oxides and a binder onto paper or a flexible plastic material. Once transferred onto the object the design is made permanent by a low temperature firing.

turning – the process of trimming the excess clay from the object when leather-hard. This is achieved by attaching the vessel upside down to the centre of a potter's wheel, and shaving away unwanted clay with a sharp implement in order to define features such as the foot rim.

underglaze colours – colours which are applied onto biscuit ware and then coated with a transparent glaze.

unfired decoration – cold-curing decoration such as paint and gold leaf which is just applied to the surface of the object without any subsequent firing. Such decoration tends to be very vulnerable to wear and environmental factors. In the presence of moisture it may dissolve or start to lift and flake away from the surface.

vitrification – the point during the firing at which the fluxes and free silica in the body become glassy and start to flow among the clay particles. Beyond this stage the body will start to deform and distort under its own weight.

APPENDIX 5

Directory of materials, terms and processes

abrasives – generally used for removing and smoothing excess from fillings and retouched areas. They consist of fine particles of materials such as silicone carbide, glass, garnet, quartz and aluminium oxide, graded according to size and hardness. The particles are usually bound onto a substrate such as paper, plastic or cloth, or, alternatively, made up as a paste or cream. In the context of cleaning, they can also be used airborne as an air abrasive, sometimes directed under pressure with a jet of water. Great care has to be taken when using abrasives in close proximity to glazed surfaces to avoid scratching the object.

acetone (propanone or dimethyl ketone) – a solvent which is both highly flammable and volatile. It has various uses: removal of dirt and grease, dissolving and removing unwanted coatings and adhesives, as a solvent for the resins during application (e.g., Paraloid B-72). The vapour is slightly toxic so inhalation should be avoided. Appropriate personal protective equipment should be worn in accordance with the manufacturer's health and safety guidelines.

acrylic paint – readily available pre-mixed paint which consists of an emulsion of various acrylic resins combined with water, pigments and extenders. They are often used for retouching fills, particularly on earthenwares. Some can be difficult to abrade and rub down, and show slight colour alteration on drying. They have good ageing properties and present little risk to the health of the user (e.g., Cryla Colours by Rowney, Winsor & Newton's acylic paints, Liquitex by Lefranc and Bourgeois, and Golden Acrylics by Golden).

acrylic resins – a large group of synthetic polymers based on the methacrylate group of polymers. They include various adhesives, coatings and casting resins which share properties of good clarity and resistance to ageing. Examples include Paraloid (Acryloid) B-72 and B-67, cyanoacrylate adhesives (so-called superglue).

adhesive tape – pressure-sensitive tape which is composed of a tape, usually clear plastic film or paper, coated on one side with tacky adhesive. The adhesive is generally some kind of viscous rubber-based resin with a low molecular weight. They provide an excellent means of support for keeping assembled fragments in position while the main resin cures.

aggregates – inert powders added as bulking materials to thicken and alter the textural and optical qualities of a resin so that, as a filling material, it imitates the physical properties of the ceramic more closely.

alkyd resins – a component of some types of paint. They are the products of reactions between polyhydric alcohols and certain organic acids. They tend to be relatively stable and resistant to yellowing in daylight. White spirit and other hydrocarbons are used as solvents for application. They set by evaporation of the solvent and gradual cross-linking (e.g., Intenso Colours).

ammonia solution – ammonium hydroxide solution (NH_4OH), a strong alkali. Used as a catalyst with hydrogen peroxide for bleaching organic dirt.

artists' pigments – coloured organic or inorganic dry powders. Although insoluble in most solvents, they can be used to colour resins.

biological washing powders – domestic washing powders, designed for cleaning clothes, containing (among other ingredients) various enzymes which help to speed up the reactions involved in dissolving dirt. They have been used to successfully clean porcelain ingrained with dirt. However, they should not be used on porous or unstable ceramics due to the risk of absorption and irreversible damage (examples include Ariel made by Proctor and Gamble, and Biotex manufactured by Blumoller).

bleach – a chemical that will remove unwanted colour by oxidation or reduction reactions.

cellulose nitrate – nitrocellulose is widely used as an adhesive and consolidant for ceramics, especially archaeological wares and earthenwares. The thermoplastic adhesive can be obtained ready-mixed with solvents in a tube; it can be further diluted or removed with acetone. It is water white, discolouring to yellow brown on ageing. Conservators should be aware that an undesirable discolouring reaction occurs between traces of cellulose nitrate adhesive and epoxy resins. Examples include HMG (Guest), Durofix (Rawlplug) and Duco Cement (Devcon).

consolidant – a resin that is applied to give strength to a weakened structure.

cyanoacrylates – *see* superglue

deionised water – water which has had ionic and organic contaminants removed as a result of being passed through a set of ion exchange resins or filters. It is not as pure as distilled water.

dental wax sheets – thin sheets of pink wax used by dentists. An impression or support material which is readily softened in hot water or with a hot-air blower.

dichloromethane (methylene dichloride) – a major component in paint strippers (e.g., Nitromors made by Wilcot and Zynolyte (USA)). It is commonly used to aid the removal of paint or adhesive. The serious adverse health risks associated with the solvent (it is a suspected carcinogen) mean that its use is likely to be banned in the future.

distilled water – chemically pure water which is produced as a result of boiling water, collecting and condensing the resulting steam.

enzymes – biological catalysts that speed up the complex reactions that take place in nature while remaining unchanged themselves. They are specific in their action and optimum performance is determined by pH and temperature. Examples include protease responsible for the breakdown of protein, and lipase which breaks down fats.

epoxy – thermosetting resins composed of a resin component and a second component which acts as a hardener. Due to their extreme strength, epoxy resins are used as adhesives and fillers on more durable non-porous wares such as stoneware and porcelain. Epoxy hardeners are toxic and extremely sensitising to the skin and respiratory system; health and safety guidelines should be followed closely. Examples include HXTAL NYL-1 (Conservator's Emporium), Araldite 2020 (Ciba-Geigy), UHU-plus endfest 300 (UHU) and Fynebond (Fyne Conservation Services).

ethanol – commonly referred to as 'alcohol', it is a highly flammable solvent and forms a major component of IMS (industrial methylated spirits). Useful for removing grease and dissolving shellac.

fumed silica – a finely divided colloidal form of synthetic silica used both as a means of thickening and opacifying epoxy resins as well as a matting agent in retouching media. Available in a hydrophobic and hydrophillic form. Examples include Cab-o-sil (Calbot), Aerosil 200 and Aerosil TT600 (Degussa).

glass transition temperature – (Tg) the temperature at which a resin starts to change from a hard and brittle material to a soft one.

gold materials – applied in various ways as gold leaf, powder gold, gold paint and tablet gold.

hydrogen peroxide – (H_2O_2) a strong oxidising agent which is used as a bleach to remove organic stains from ceramics. It breaks down during the reaction to form water and active oxygen. It is available in various strengths, although the full strength 100 volumes (30% solution) has to be obtained from specialist suppliers. Ammonia solution is often used as a catalyst, speeding up the release of oxygen.

IMS – (industrial methylated spirits) consists mainly of ethanol with a small amount of methanol (approx. 9.5%) and water. It represents a cheaper alternative to ethanol which is purer and in the UK is supplied under special licence. Ordinary methylated spirits, which is readily available in pharmacists, is not suitable for conservation as it contains a purple dye as well as the solvent pyridine. IMS may reverse shellac bonds and is also a useful cleaning agent and degreasant.

Laponite RD – a very fine white powder consisting of a synthetic silicate manufactured from pure chemicals, closely allied to natural clay minerals. It is used as a poulticing material to remove stains from ceramics, stone, paintings, metal, textiles and other organic materials. For application it is carefully stirred into deionised water (approx. 5% by weight), left to stand for 30 minutes then stirred again. After a few hours a clear thixotropic colloidal gel is formed. The gel is spread onto the surface of the previously soaked ceramic and left to draw out the stain. The gel may also be combined with other solvents. Manufacturer's health and safety guidelines should be consulted

latex – rubber latex is a naturally occurring material which is cheap and readily available. It is used as a highly flexible moulding material. It usually contains ammonia to give it enhanced stability, and is pre-vulcanised by the addition of sulphur to produce a cross-linked product. Moulds can be reinforced by adding cotton flock or gauze to the liquid latex, and petroleum jelly can be used as a release agent.

lustre pigments – non-metallic powders consisting of very small transparent particles of mica coated in titanium dioxide or iron oxide (e.g., Mearlite made by Mearl).

matting agents – materials added to retouching media to remove their gloss. Micronised silica gels are often used to produce matt effects.

Nitromors – *see* dichloromethane.

non-ionic detergent – a purified cleaning product containing a non-ionic surfactant which lowers the surface tension of water and aids cleaning by emulsifying and solubilising grease and dirt. Widely used for general cleaning, a few drops (0.2% by volume) are added to water to make it 'wetter' (e.g., Synperonic A7 and Synperonic 91/6 (ICI)).

Paraloid – called Acryloid in the USA – a proprietary brand of resins (produced by Rohm and Haas, USA). There are several different types available. The most commonly used are B-72, an ethyl methacrylate methyl acrylate copolymer, and B-67, an isobutyl methacrylate polymer.

plaster of Paris (calcium sulphate hemihydrate) – when mixed with water it sets by exothermic reaction to form a hard, white solid with a similar density to that of ceramic bodies. It is available in various grades which vary in particle size, setting time expansion and colour. Those grades designed for use by the dental profession tend to be favoured by ceramics conservators. Disadvantages include the short working time, expansion on setting, difficulty of removal and the risk of sulphate salts at a later stage.

polishing creams – pastes, creams or liquids consisting of a mixture of solvents, emulsifiers and waxes in which very fine particles of abrasive are suspended (e.g., Solvol Autochrome by Hammerite).

polyester – thermosetting liquids used as adhesives and fillers consisting of a mixture of an unsaturated polyester and styrene. A prepolymer of low molecular weight is mixed with a peroxide-based initiator. There are various types available which are used as adhesives and gap-fillers. As adhesives, they can prove useful where mechanical joins are required, for instance on a large heavy object. Some of the adhesives are fast setting and this can also be an advantage (e.g., General by General Industria Chimica). The resins tend to yellow unacceptably with age. The styrene component in the uncured resin is highly toxic and the peroxide part can also cause irritation and sensitisation. Great care should be taken when mixing and handling polyesters, and the advice given on the manufacturer's health and safety data sheets should be followed closely.

Polyfilla – a proprietary decorator's filler (made by Polycell), available in various grades, consisting of modified mixtures of plaster of Paris. The All Purpose grade of Polyfilla is sold as a powder which has to be mixed with water for application and consists of plaster of Paris reinforced with cellulose. Fine Surface Polyfilla is a ready-mixed fine grade filler used only for fine cracks and shallow irregularities (due to its shrinkage), consisting of a vinyl acetate copolymer mixed with inorganic mineral fillers and thickeners.

polymer – an organic molecule consisting of a long chain of hundreds or thousands of smaller units.

polyurethane – resins which were previously popular as retouching mediums. They are the product of an alcohol and an isocyanate group resin. Although the resins have good working properties, the cured resin tends to yellow rapidly in daylight. The risk to health and safety from the highly toxic isocyanates released during the curing reaction have reduced the popularity of this resin and all data sheets should be carefully consulted before use.

poly(vinyl acetate) – PVAC, a vinyl polymer, widely used as an adhesive in various conservation applications as an aqueous emulsion. It also has other uses as a consolidant, coating and gap-filler. Unfortunately its low glass transition temperature of around room temperature would make its use inappropriate in hot climates, except where air conditioning could be guaranteed. The resin is soluble in warm water, acetone, ethanol and toluene. In time it will cross-link to some extent, making removal impossible. Examples include: Mowilith DMC2 (Hoechst), Jade (Aabitt), PVA AYAF (Union Carbide) and Evo-stik Wood Adhesive Resin W (Evode).

poly(vinyl alcohol) – PVAL, a copolymer of vinyl alcohol and vinyl acetate. The resin is sometimes used as a consolidant for unstable surfaces and as a separating layer on moulding materials. While readily soluble in water, it will only dissolve in a small number of organic solvents. The resin has good ageing properties. Examples include Gelvatol (Monsanto), Mowiol (Hoechst) and Polyviol (Wacker).

poulticing material – an inert material which is mixed with a solvent to form a soft paste and applied to the surface of an object in order to remove unwanted stains, salts or deposits. The poultice holds the solvent in very close contact with the object enabling it to dissolve the unwanted substance. As the solvent evaporates, the stains are drawn from the pores of the ceramic into the poultice. Examples of materials that have been successfully used on ceramics include Laponite RD, Sepiolite, attapulgite, methyl cellulose, paper pulp and cotton wool.

rubberised cleaning materials – are sometimes used on surfaces where it is undesirable to introduce water or other liquids. Ingrained surface dirt can be removed from unglazed porous surfaces. Various erasers designed for use on paper will also work quite effectively on some types of dirt on ceramic surfaces. Examples include: the Staedtler Mars Plastic eraser, Kneadable Putty Rubber (Daler Rowney), Draft Clean (Arcesso); however, they may leave undesirable residues on porous surfaces.

sequestering agent – a chemical compound which is able to form complexes with metal ions, separating them and making them soluble, enabling them to be safely removed. Ethylene diamine tetra-acetic acid (EDTA) has been successfully used for this purpose.

shellac, bleached – a resin derived from a secretion of the lac insects occurring in South Asia. It was popular in the past as an adhesive for repairing broken ceramics despite its inappropriate colour, poor ageing properties and lack of reversibility. It can be problematical to remove due to its increasing insolubility with age. However, as a coating it is still used with some success for retouching fillings on some earthenware and archaeological ceramics.

silicone rubber – a silicone-based polymer which is used to make moulds. A catalyst has to be mixed with the rubber for curing to occur. There are various types: some are quick-setting impression materials that have a putty-like consistency, while others are viscous liquids which can be poured. They will reproduce surface detail with a high level of accuracy. Tests should be made before use to ensure that there is no risk of damage to the object; some may stain porous earthenware due to their oil content and others may transfer colouring material.

superglue – the common name for cyanoacrylate acrylic adhesives. They are used to provide (almost) instant bonds. They are not widely used in conservation as their long-term stability and reversibility is uncertain. They can, however, be useful for situations where there is no other means of attaching and supporting components during curing, such as delicate decorative details.

talc – hydrated magnesium silicate, or French chalk. It can be mixed into epoxy resins to thicken and bulk them, producing an opaque filling. Also added to retouching media to fill small surface irregularities.

thermoplastic resins – resins which can be softened by repeated heating without changing their properties. They are usually soluble in solvents (e.g., acrylics, PVAs and wax).

thermosetting resins – polymers which have a three-dimensional structure with cross-links between the chains. They are usually formed from two-part resins where a cross-linking agent or hardener is mixed with a resin composed of long chains (e.g., epoxy resins and silicone rubber).

titanium dioxide – a fine-textured dense white pigment with good hiding properties. It is used to whiten retouching media and filling materials.

urea formaldehyde – a resin from the formaldehyde group which is used as a retouching medium. They are highly cross-linked network polymers produced by reacting a resin component with a catalyst. The coating is very hard and brittle and can be abraded and polished as necessary (e.g., Rustins Plastic Coating). Manufacturer's health and safety guidelines should be consulted and the risks associated with inhalation avoided by use of local exhaust ventilation.

white spirit – a hydrocarbon solvent composed mainly of aliphatic molecules as well as some aromatic and alicyclic molecules. It is a useful solvent for oils, grease, fat, wax, tar and some resins. Health and safety guidelines should be followed closely during use.

APPENDIX 6

Conservation associations and other bodies

American Institute for Conservation (AIC), 1717 K Street, N.W., Suite 200, Washington, DC 20006, USA

Canadian Conservation Institute (CCI), 1030 Innes Road, Ottawa, K1A 0M5, Canada

The Getty Conservation Institute, 1200 Getty Center Drive, Suite 700, Los Angeles, CA 90049-1684, USA

Health and Safety Executive, Rose Court, 2 Southwark Bridge, London SE1 9HS, UK

Heritage Care Association, c/o NRLC, Sector E-3, Aliganj Scheme, Lucknow 226024, India

Indian Association for the Study of Conservation of Cultural Property, c/o National Museum, Janpath, New Delhi 110001, India

INTACH Indian Conservation Institute, B-42, Nirala Nagar, Lucknow – 226 020, India

International Centre for the Study and the Preservation and Restoration of Cultural Material (ICCROM), 13 Via di S. Michele, Rome 1-00153, Italy

International Council of Museums (ICOM), Conservation Committee Working Group for Glass, Ceramics and Related Materials, Maison de l'Unesco, 1 Rue Miollis, 75732 Paris CEDEX 15, France

International Institute for Conservation (IIC), 6 Buckingham Street, London WC2N 6BA, UK

National Research Laboratory for Conservation of Cultural Property (NRLC), Government of India Department of Culture, Sector E/3, Aliganj Scheme, Lucknow 226024, India

United Kingdom Institute for Conservation (UKIC), Ceramics and Glass Conservation Group, 109 The Chandlery, 50 Westminster Bridge Road, London SE1 7QD, UK